Particular Bravery

The Battle of Xa Cam My
and
The Death of a Grunt Company

T. L. Derks

BookLocker
Trenton, Georgia

Copyright © 2023 T. L. Derks

Paperback ISBN: 978-1-958877-98-2
Hardcover ISBN: 978-1-958877-99-9
Ebook ISBN: 979-8-88531-362-9

All rights reserved. No part of this publication may be reproduced, stored in a retrieval system, or transmitted in any form or by any means, electronic, mechanical, recording or otherwise, without the prior written permission of the author.

Published by BookLocker.com, Inc., Trenton, Georgia.

Library of Congress Cataloging in Publication Data
Derks, T. L.
Particular Bravery; The Battle of Xa Cam My and the Death of a Grunt Company by T. L. Derks
Library of Congress Control Number: 2022918667

Printed on acid-free paper.

Booklocker.com, Inc
2023

First Edition

Cover Photo: Public Domain, courtesy of John Libs—photo of John Libs in Vietnam.
Back Cover Photo: Paid Consideration, The Associated Press, LIC-01459468

"It doesn't require any particular bravery to stand on the floor of the Senate and urge our boys in Vietnam to fight harder, and if…a hundred thousand young Americans are killed, it won't be U.S. Senators who die. It will be American soldiers who are too young to qualify for the senate."

George McGovern

Dedication

To my loving wife, Barbara, who helped in ways she knows and in ways she does not know. Without you, this book would have been impossible.

Table of Contents

Preface: War is Vulgar xv
Prologue: The Roar 1
Chapter One: Easter 9
Chapter Two: Walking Point 25
Chapter Three: Roll up the Wagons 63
Chapter Four: The Descent 91
Photos 115
Chapter Five: "A Serious Blow" 119
Chapter Six: The Longest Night 151
Chapter Seven: The Mornings After 175
Epilogue: The Reunion, 2001 201
Charlie Company, 2/16, 1st Infantry
    Division Interviewees 209
The Fallen Americans of Xa Cam My 211
Bibliography 213

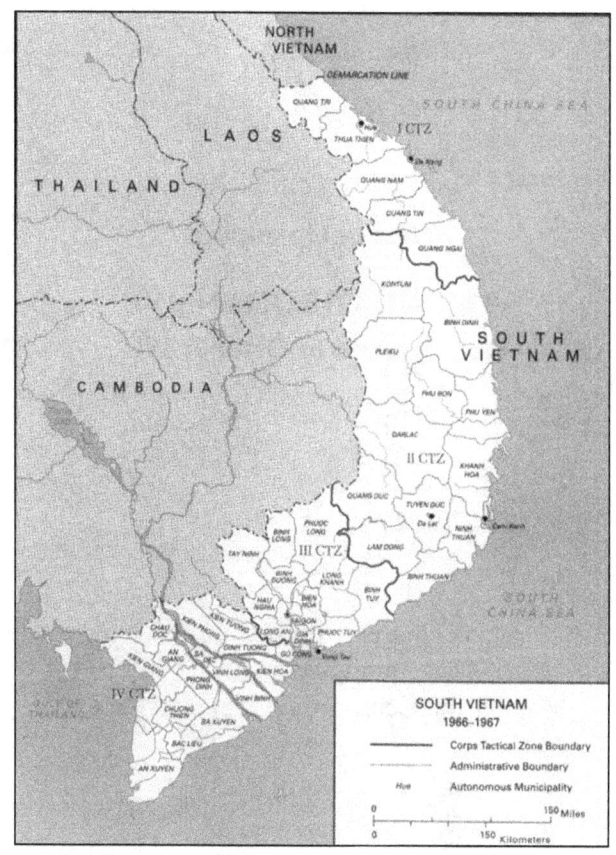

Military Regions in South Vietnam, 1966-67
Public Domain
George L. MacGarrigle, The United States Army in Vietnam: Combat Operations, Taking the Offensive, October 1966- October 1967. Washington DC: Center of Military History, 1998.

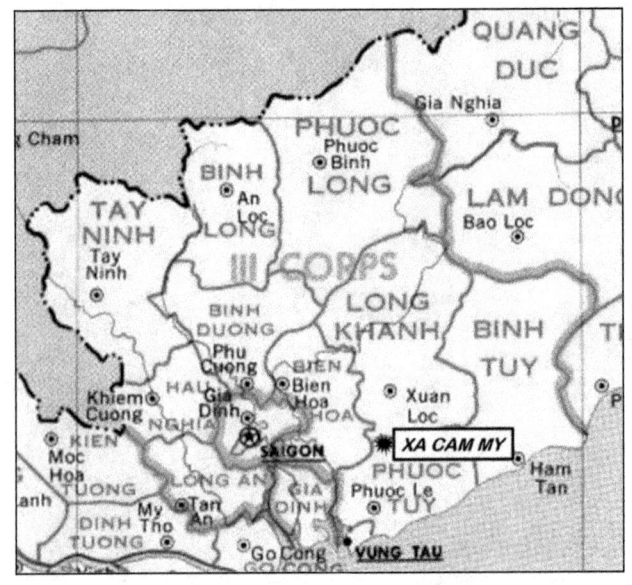

III Corps with battle site
Public Domain
Map by the Central Intelligence Agency.

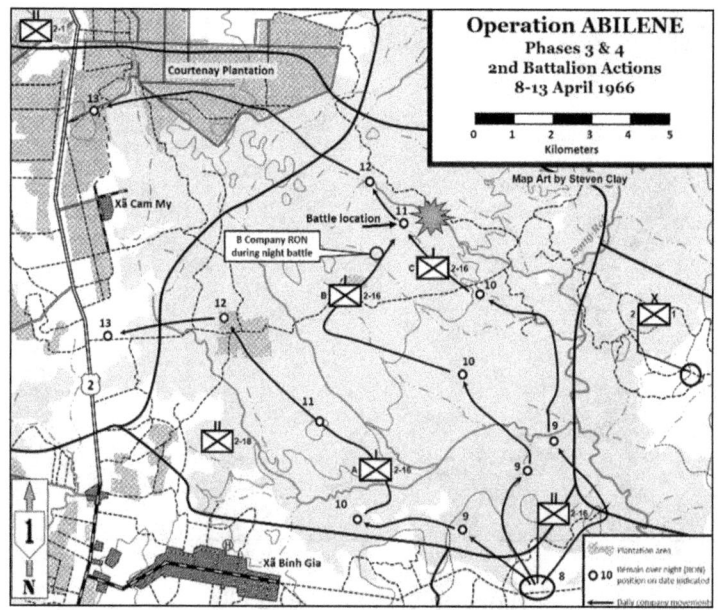

Map courtesy of Steven Clay

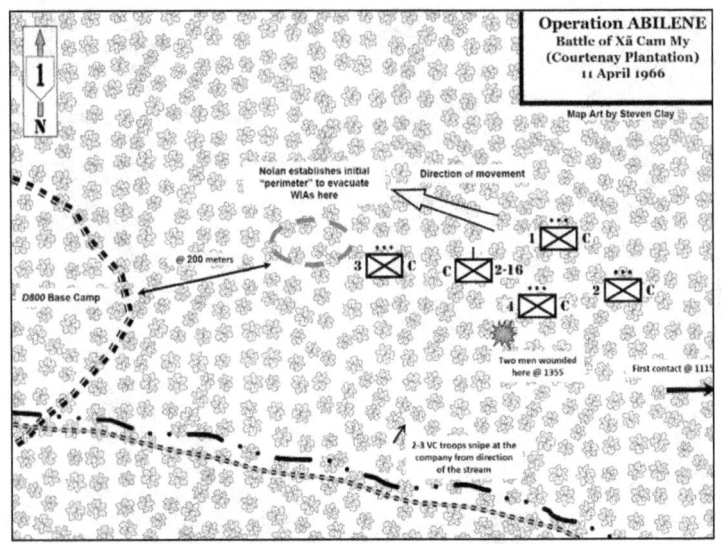

Map courtesy of Steve Clay

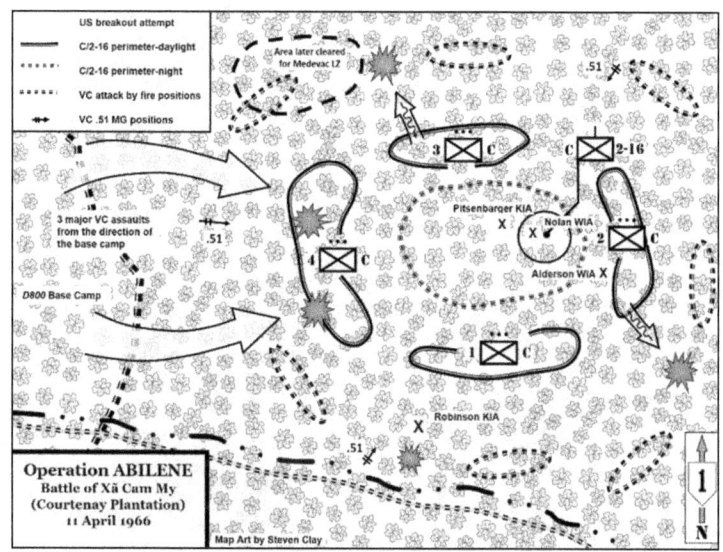

Map courtesy of Steve Clay

Preface:
War is Vulgar

"War is the most vulgar thing human beings can do to one another. You can't prepare someone for that."

> *Survivor of the Battle*

"Vietnam is a land of smiles."

> *Gary McKay, Australia's Battlefields in Viet Nam*

This is the story of a battle fought in April 1966, between a company of United States soldiers and Viet Cong forces near a village called Xa Cam My forty miles east of Saigon. It was not a large battle as such things are measured, there was no grand maneuvering on the battlefield by army corps or divisions. There was no unit larger than a regiment on the field of battle, and the total combatants from both sides probably did not exceed eight hundred. There was no strategic worth to the engagement. The battle did not change the course of the war for the victors or the vanquished. For American commanders, it was a small calamity on a nightmarish and claustrophobic patch of blood-soaked dirt.

Still, there are reasons enough to look at the battle. One reason is to shed light on potential causes for an American military defeat that General William Westmoreland labeled "a serious blow."[1] The Army Chief of Staff at the time, General Harold K. Johnson had his doubts about Westmoreland's strategy for fighting the war. The battle did nothing to convince Johnson differently, even prompting him to fly to Vietnam after the fight to dress down General DePuy (the First Division's commander at the time of the battle) and by extension, warn Westmoreland that his strategy was faulty, bloody. "You know, The American people won't support this war if we keep having the kind of casualties suffered by Charlie Company."

Another objective in studying the battle is to weave the veterans' subjective memories of that particular combat into a cohesive narrative of the battle. It is also worth noting that by looking at this battle much of what was typical of combat in the early years of the Vietnam War comes into focus. But mostly this book exists because these men's stories, as much as possible, need to be preserved for the historical record. Some were heroes, some were cowards, and some were both heroes and cowards. They were all soldiers of the United States who were sent to fight in Southeast Asia by men in the halls of power who demonstrated no particular bravery in ordering these soldiers to fight.

Operation ABILENE involved elements of the United States Army's First Infantry Division in a search-and-destroy campaign during the spring of 1966. The operation was designed to disrupt planned Viet Cong offensives targeting Saigon. For this operation the First Division's commander, General William DePuy, broke his command down into its constituent parts, with no unit larger than an infantry company slopping through the jungle together; enticing guerillas to strike, thus enabling the general to unleash artillery on the enemy. Unfortunately for the men of Company C, 2nd Battalion, 16th Regiment, DePuy's plan was predicated on American units being alone but within swift marching distance of supporting units, and when Company C (Charlie Company) was caught out of position on April 11, 1966, the results were disastrous for the Americans.

This book explores the actions of C Company personnel during the operation that culminated in their near annihilation in the vicinity of the village of Xa Cam My, Phuoc Tuy Province, which sits between what was then the capital city of South Vietnam, Saigon, and the South China Sea.

This is a combat narrative, a recollection of a battle America did not win and the story, from their imperfect memories, of the Americans who fought that battle. It is not a work about strategy or tactics. It is about men impaled on the sharp end of the spear of war.

In approaching the work in this manner, I also encountered a phenomenon identified by Vietnam memoirist and novelist Tim O'Brien: the "truth" of Vietnam War stories. In his memoir *The Things They Carried*, O'Brien warns the reader not to dismiss a Vietnam veteran's war story because it seems fanciful or unbelievable. He contends that in a true war story "...it's difficult to separate what happened from what *seemed* to happen. [Italics added] What seems to happen becomes its own happening and has to be told that way." O'Brien further contends that this "seemingness" of an event in Vietnam is as real and true as what might have happened objectively. To the man who recalls a particular story, his version is always the truth, while fifty other witnesses may remember it differently.[2] Early on in drafting this book, I determined that where one veteran's "seeming" truth about a particular event conflicted with another man's truth, each man's account would be recorded without judging whose story was correct.

The story of the battle is an amalgamation of the individual truths of dozens of survivors, but it is not the final truth. A complete accounting of the battle would have to include the truths of every combatant. This is impossible for obvious reasons. Instead, a partial retelling of some American combatants' experiences makes up this work.

Combat is chaos. Participants and historians will agree on that. Certainly, there may be careful planning that precedes combat, with well-defined objectives and clear expectations laid down in pre-operational plans, but strategists' plans and objectives do not define combat. Neither does the scholar's careful research and meticulous literary reconstruction of a battle do more than impose order on what is by nature disorderly. Chaos is a better definition. Pandemonium, the wild horror within the devil's charnel house might be closer to the truth. At least regarding this combat, in that place, on that day, for those men.

Combat is dirty and ambiguous – that is a truth as well.

Yet, it is the military historian's task to convey some of the truth of combat, that cauldron of bloody negative experiences, while also piecing together a pattern or at least a narrative flow in which those bloody negative experiences occurred. Finding that pattern and melding it into a presentation of the truth of combat as the men of Charlie Company, 2/16, experienced it is my objective in writing about the Battle of Xa Cam My.

To complete this work, it was necessary to arrange source material into three distinct groups; first are personal recollections of battle survivors; second is the official documentation; and third is the various media write-ups or reports of the battle, along with some secondary published materials.

This narrative will emphasize the personal recollections of the survivors. Though the narrative contains the elements of a traditional combat narrative—in fact, relies on those elements—it also possesses the traits of the Vietnam memoir, but magnified through the combination of the survivors' voices.

The official documentation referred to above has been obtained from the National Archives in Maryland and Missouri, the First Infantry Division's Museum at Cantigny Park, in Illinois, the 16th Infantry Regiment Association, and the survivors' private collections.

Survivors were contacted by snail mail, phone, and e-mail. Initially, I was aided in these contacts through the good offices of a Charlie Company veteran who had established a website for the battle's survivors. He was responsible for many introductions, and without those introductions, some of the veterans would not have interacted with me. I am grateful for his assistance and at his request, he remains anonymous.

For the most part, interviews were conducted over the phone. The interviews were taped, and those tapes remain in my possession. I asked some basic biographical questions to begin the interview and to make the interviewee comfortable, then I let the individual tell me what he wanted known about the battle. Certainly, some questions came up because of an individual's recollections, but these questions varied with the particular veteran and presented no effort on my part to elicit information that I had predetermined as necessary for the story. This method meant that an individual's story did not always mesh with other participants' recollections. These inconsistencies are a cost of the confusion of battle and the unique nature of a soldier's piece of the war. Again, to reference Tim O'Brien, war stories are what the individual remembers, however unbelievable, because to the man telling it, the man remembering it, "…it happened. Because every word is absolutely dead-on true."[3]

In some ways, these mismatched stories make the whole account of the battle more accurate. For if combat is chaos and blood then discrepancies do not negate the shape of battle but confirm it. The men of Charlie Company had their share of chaos and blood on April 11, 1966, and though their particular piece of that chaos may differ from the pieces remembered by other veterans, they are all part of the true story of the Battle of Xa Cam My.

..

For assorted reasons this project has taken much longer to complete than I anticipated would be the case as I began it. The responsibility for the long duration between the research's beginning and the manuscript's completion is entirely mine. My biggest regret regarding this book is that many of the men interviewed passed away before they could read the finished story.

My gratitude to the many people who trusted me with their stories or assisted with finding material has not dimmed with those long years between the project's start-up and its completion here. The vision upon setting out on this project was to tell the story of men in a desperate nightmare and now I find

I have written about the nightmare of so many of my friends. For I count the men of Company C as my friends.

In 2005, a shorter version of this research was presented as my Master's thesis at Sam Houston State University. Much of the work here is based on that thesis, though the manuscript has been altered and new information appears throughout. So, a hardy thank you goes to my thesis committee, Professors Ty Cashion, and Nicholas Pappas. And a special thank you to Professor James S. Olson. His patience was incredible, and his suggestions, though not always heeded, were appreciated.

Of course, all the veterans of Charlie Company that allowed me to interview them have my gratitude. Men relived some of the worst moments of their lives in these interviews and everyone I spoke with gave me some information that could be used in this retelling. Rather than clutter the story with citations for these interviews I have listed the veterans at the back of the book. If a story describes a particular soldier, it is that man that told me the story. A partial bibliography of the secondary works and primary material follows the interviewee list.

I also want to thank the editorial staff at *Vietnam* magazine, especially David T. Zabecki, who, in the early 2000s, published my 4000-word article concerning the battle.

Stephen Hawkins and Andrew Woods of the First Infantry Division Museum also encouraged my work and Woods' article on the battle added important insights to my understanding of certain individuals' actions in the turmoil of combat. This is also true of the president of the 16th Infantry Regiment Association, Steven Clay, who is the author of the excellent history of the 16th Infantry Regiment, *Blood and Sacrifice*. Twenty years ago, he took the time to sketch out a map overlay of the route taken by Company C as they trudged through the jungle toward their destiny. He did this despite a time crunch because he was preparing to leave for South Korea for a year.

Twenty years later Steve once again took time from his own projects to create a set of maps based on his earlier work but adapted to meet my publisher's requirements.

Then there is George C. Wilson, now deceased, who blazed the trail with C Company. His book, *Mud Soldiers, Life Inside the New American Army*, though not focused on the Battle of Xa Cam My, used the fight as a jumping-off point to look at how the U.S. Army had changed since the Vietnam War. Limited though his account of the battle is, it is an important precursor for my account of the battle.

Each of the veterans who took the time to share their stories have my eternal gratitude and thanks. As I mentioned earlier, I consider each of them a friend. However, a few of the Charlie Company alum warrants my special attention because they went above and beyond. First, there is Phil Hall, who kept encouraging me. He helped with introductions and regimental connections. Bob Fisher, who said my words "went to the heart of the matter." Ken Mize helped me in the beginning and at the end of this journey. The late Dave Burris, whose story drew me in and has never let me go—Dave was patient with me as I pestered him for clarifications and more, always more. There is Roger Harris, who shared his manuscript "Charlie's Kid" with me, and a hundred tidbits that kept me on the right track. John Libs, the cocky young lieutenant from 1966, his stories all reflect his protective nature toward his men. And, the late Marty Kroah, who was everyone's idea of a soldier.

Prologue: The Roar

"True war stories do not generalize. They do not indulge in abstraction or analysis... A true war story, if truly told, makes the stomach believe."

Tim O'Brien, The Things They Carried.

The roar. The great howling of the enemy's fire, the friendlies' return fire, the mortars, and the artillery careening in from overhead; these sounds engulfed Pfc Dave Burris as he huddled behind the questionable cover of a log that seemed to be the target for all that munitions and noise. Plus, there was the screaming. Sergeant Schoolman. The sergeant was bellowing orders to the other men of the squad, prone behind that log, the line of defense, a downed tree midway down a jungled slope. Burris was amazed that he could hear Schoolman over the wall of noise that gripped the area. In addition to that cacophony of chaos, a .51 caliber Chicom machine gun was throwing slugs against the exposed side of the log, chewing systematically at the wood, and that weapon added its thick snarl to the roar. From the sound of things, Burris was sure the gun was firing from point-blank range.

Burris, a genuine 11bullet stopper*, was alone at the end of the log. The lieutenant was missing; the platoon sergeant was dead. Seasholtz, the fire team leader, was down. Schoolman was close by, there beyond another trooper, but Burris could see, could unbelievably *hear*, the sergeant directing his attention to the squad that stretched out to his right—away from Burris at the end of the log. And the trooper nearest Burris, just an arm's length distance to the right, was focused on Schoolman, leaving Burris alone at the end of the log.

Burris knew that somewhere outside the slim protection of the log lay the safety of the 2nd Brigade's base camp at Bear Cat on Highway 2. A native of Redwood City, California, the Pfc, however, did not know at that moment in which direction that particular mass of mud and barbed wire lay. He did not know that the log and the company, and unfortunately, he, were all forty miles east of Saigon, between the capital city of South Vietnam and the South China Sea. Besides, knowing any of that was not going to help get him through the fight.

It was Burris' lonely Vietnam War of 1966. His war at the end of the log, the end of the line in Phuoc Tuy Province that held the May Tao Secret Zone, an area where until a couple of weeks before this nightmare afternoon, the Vietcong had reigned unchallenged by U.S. military power. The end of the line for Burris and the 3rd platoon of Charlie Company and the "Rangers" of the 2nd Battalion, 16th Regiment, First Infantry Division. Burris crammed another clip into his M16 and prayed that the log would hold since he *was* the end of the line.

Then there was the dirt splattering into the Californian's face. The ground out beyond the deadfall, the exposed earth to the Pfc's left, was belching up dirt clots that were smacking him in the face. Someone was shooting at Burris not only to his front but from out on the left. He jerked his rifle up to his shoulder and drew a bead at the space beyond his left. A Viet Cong was visible about twenty yards off firing at the American. Luckily the VC was firing too low, churning up the ground. Burris retaliated with a burst. The firing from that direction stopped.

Having knocked off the VC Burris was not comforted. He was surveying the ground beyond the left of the log, and out there on the left, on that gently sloping ground, moments before – minutes before, who could tell in a firefight – a squad from 4th Platoon had protected 3rd Platoon's left flank. But when Burris scanned that ground in the moments after firing at the VC, the Pfc saw nothing in that direction but great gouges in the earth, clipped branches, and dead bodies. 4th Platoon had pulled out, had been forced out, or wiped out. Burris was the flank.

It was then that Burris added his cry to the roar of combat. "Our left flank is exposed. I'm getting fire." He howled at Sergeant Schoolman. Schoolman registered the new situation.

"Pull back. Get up the hill. Form a perimeter up the hill!"

Anywhere uphill, up that slight incline, was exposed ground. Burris saw that immediately. He was afraid to move, but he knew he could not stay behind that log; to remain in his position meant death. He and the other members of the squad started a frantic crawl up the slope.

Flat against the ground, flat against the churned-up dirt, shattered earth slick with blood. A trooper further up the slope than Burris—a trooper between Burris and safety. Slow, painfully slow. "Come on, move, move." Crack. Fire from the left. Crack. From the right. "Move!" "I can't, I'm hit." No time to help the guy. Scrambled over him. Left him. Burris flopped behind a tree. The roar followed.

Burris swung his M16 around and provided covering fire. The wounded trooper managed to crawl behind another upright tree about three yards to Burris' right. Another grunt, John "Ollie" Lang, reached Burris' perch. Lang went prone behind the tree. The trees were five or six feet in diameter. Awful small for hiding two bodies. Behind the other tree, the tree that protected the wounded soldier; a cluster of busted-up GIs. The Californian watched as these men squirmed for position, pressed in to avoid the sheet of bullets pouring in on the squad. Bark flew off the tree, the air between the trees whirring with lead, and the ground on both sides of the tree flayed with machine gun fire. A mortar round exploded nearby. Lang was hit with shrapnel.

"You got room over there?" shouted an exposed soldier from behind the tree where the wounded troopers crowded together. "No, no." Burris wailed back, but Lang waved the man over. Somehow Richard Garner made it through the hail of bullets to land between Lang and Burris.

"They're in the trees," someone called. Burris looked up, thought he saw flashes and threw some rounds into the trees.

He was satisfied that he saw no more flashes from those particular trees.

Off to the right and the rear of Burris' position, Sergeant Schoolman screamed, "I'm hit." Farther off to the right, the racket told Burris that third Platoon's other squads were being kicked apart. The perimeter had cracked; now, the men simply huddled behind trees and waited to die. Burris stared up at the canopy of broken branches and hanging limbs. There was tear gas caught in the branches, adding to the shadows of the coming darkness.

"God, I've got to piss," Burris said aloud. In combat, under fire, and with no room to maneuver, the Californian needed to void his bladder.

Garner, always one to crack a joke: "Well, stand up then." For a moment, the roar was replaced with laughter, but only for a moment. Then Burris was slammed by a bullet. The impact hurled the Pfc from behind the tree. Immediately the air around him thickened with aimed fire. Burris scrambled back behind the tree.

Garner was groaning. Burris could see that Garner had been hit near the base of the spine, and the bullet had exited Garner and continued toward Burris, where it bashed into an ammunition pouch on Burris' right hip. Garner's body had provided a margin of cushion that bled the bullet of its force before it reached Burris. The bullet had not penetrated the skin. Still, the impact had thrown Burris from behind cover and supplied some desperate moments as he hustled back to the tree.

Then the roar thinned. Thinned, broke. Less firing from the front, fewer moans, and wails from the right—from behind the tree where so many wounded sought refuge. Not quiet, but a softening of the din.

With darkness closing in, a new and terrifying horror crept onto the battlefield. The incoming fire had diminished. The gunfire was replaced by a woeful sound, a maddening sound ripping at Burris' psyche—the tormented calls of the wounded outside the perimeter.

Randall "Peanuts" Prinz lay somewhere in the no-man's-land in front of 3rd Platoon, and from that horrid landscape, he called out for his friend Richard Garner. For the three soldiers pinned behind the tree, the thought of Prinz hurt and beyond reach was maddening. "Garner, I'm hit," Prinz would call out. Lang hollered back, "Hold on, Peanuts, I'm coming," though the bullets and his wounds kept him from moving. Garner and Burris offered shouts of encouragement, but they were unable to help their friend. Finally, the cries for help dwindled to nothing.

Full dark. Lang and Garner determined to pull back; find the CP. "Don't leave me here," Burris said to Lang and Garner, but they were already gone. Burris was alone again. He noticed that his legs were wet. "Am I hit?" He asked himself. He felt down around his legs. He had pissed on himself.

A new roar flared up inside Burris' head. "God damn it, I'm not going to let these guys walk over me," he told himself, referring to the enemy. He knew he was dead, there was too much death all around him to doubt that, but he was going to do something about the manner of his death.

The soldier's determination was short-circuited by another trooper's sudden appearance behind the adjacent tree—the tree where only dead lay moments before. This newcomer was carrying an M79 grenade launcher, a bloop gun. He called over to Burris, "How's it going?" Burris thought the question asinine, especially from a soldier he did not know, "How do you think it's going?" The grenadier ignored the response and fired his weapon. The grenade hit a vine about three yards in front of the tree (an M79 shell needs a few revolutions before it is armed) and bounced *back* between the two trees. The grenadier attempted to bat the threat away with the M79, swatting at the grenade with the weapon's barrel. The grenade exploded. The grenadier took shrapnel in the back, a chunk of shrapnel embedded in Burris' elbow.

Burris drifted. Passed out. Darkness was a friend.

It was the darkness that roared then. Out of the night, Burris was shaken awake when he heard a bullhorn blast Vietnamese gibberish over the battlefield. "This is it," the Pfc told himself, "the gooks must be getting ready for a final charge." Burris studied the ground around him. He was alone. He readied his weapon. There were only the voices of the enemy, some female, some laughing. He heard them moving through the brush. Then he caught American voices, weak, strained, out where the perimeter had been before the VC pushed the GIs back. The American voices said, "please, don't." He heard shots.

Soon Burris made out the sound of exploration closer to hand. The movement sounded like someone crawling through the bush. A Vietcong was slithering toward him. Burris prairie-dogged his head from behind the tree for a moment—he needed to know what was approaching him. There was a human form crawling on hands and knees toward the tree.

"Who is it?" Burris hissed.

"Perez."

Burris did not know Perez. Perez must have been from another squad. But Perez was a friendly. Perez meant Burris was not alone.

"Come on." Burris urged as he reached out from behind the tree with his left hand. Burris snatched at the collar on the other man's shirt. Burris had him.

Hollywood timing. Precise, as if staged, but real. Just as Burris gripped the man's clothing in preparation to pull him to safety, three VCs rose out of the mist behind Perez. Just stood up out of the mist and began shooting. The bullets tore into

Perez's back. Perez flopped down as Burris released him. Burris was engulfed in the roar of his M16 as he emptied the weapon at the advancing enemy.

---

* "11 bullet catcher," –11B is the military occupational specialties (MOS) for an Army infantryman. Bullet catcher was one of the many derogatory terms growing from that.

Chapter One:
Easter

"There was discussion among the officers that we had to change our positions before night because the Vietcong that got away would be reporting to Battalion D-800. We could expect mortars or even an attack. This operation was becoming as intense as predicted."

"It sure made things exciting."

Roger Harris, Pfc, 1ˢᵗ Platoon, Charlie Company.

2nd Platoon's new medic, Bob Fisher, was happy to get the rest. The medic had been in the field since he joined the company; ten days of sweat-soaked, bug-infested, vine-wrestling, heat-enduring slogging through an operation called ABILENE. Now the company had settled in along the tree line of a large clearing. The standard listening posts were laid out, but for the most part, the company was relaxing along the clearing's elephant-grass edge while waiting for the resupply helicopters—the "slicks" or "choppers"—to fly in food and ammo. Besides the supplies, one of the slicks was bringing a chaplain to deliver a late afternoon sermon on that particular day, Easter Sunday, 1966. The sermon would be Fisher's time to rest.

Fisher figured he needed the break after enduring the early look at what his war would consist of for the next year. First, he had been a heartbeat away from getting hit by friendly fire his first day in Vietnam—it was back at the repple depple (90th replacement battalion) near Bien Hoa, not even out in the field, and Fisher was leaning forward on his bunk, carrying on a conversation with a tired GI due to return to "the World," America. The GI accidentally discharged his pistol, sending a .45 slug into Fisher's new fatigues and popping a hole through his dog tags. Fatefully, Fisher had been leaning forward, and the bullet caught the bloused-out shirt and the hanging tags and not his flesh. It was going to be a long war. Then, a few days later, Fisher's first serious act as a medic was to stick his hand in some muck that moments before had been a soldier's brains; a sniper had just shot the trooper. Because it was Fisher's first soldier killed in action (KIA), the medic's adrenaline was flooding his system, preventing him from leaving the body when the medivac helicopters came roaring in. Fisher had spent a frantic chopper ride working on the guy's chest even as his hand remained mired in the exposed brain. Fisher's first KIA.

Next came the lost patrol. A squad from the 2nd Platoon wandered off one morning without a radio, stomping around the rain forest all day and in danger of spending a night isolated in the jungle. Luckily, someone in the squad had remembered that they were carrying orange signal panels, which they laid out in a clearing so a helicopter could retrieve the troops just as death at dusk was becoming a real threat. The patrolling and booby traps and gripes of a grunt company in the field compounded the misery.

Operation ABILENE was proving to be a rough breaking-in period for the medic. Fisher had heard that ABILENE was a hunt for a main force Vietcong battalion haunting the jungles east of Saigon. He was less concerned with the why of the company's mission in the field than with his exhaustion and disorientation. Fisher figured he deserved a rest.[4]

The visiting chaplain stood just inside the tree line, facing out toward the clearing with the worshippers in the clearing and facing him. Although Fisher was Catholic and the service was Protestant, he felt the need to "...get close to my priest." He was not exactly listening to the chaplain as much as gathering comfort from proximity as he took note of the other men who were not attending the service, men writing letters and cleaning their weapons. It seemed a good sign to the inexperienced Fisher that the men were so relaxed.

Dave Marchetti of Company C, 1st Medical Battalion, a medic who usually worked an aid station but who had been dragooned into the operation at the last minute, noted that the men were lulling around but quiet, not shooting the shit as he had expected. The men were anticipating a tough time in their future. Still, the day itself was surprisingly mild, even beautiful. A breeze was blowing, and the chow was hot, which was a real change for an operation. A nice day for Easter.

Pfc Roger Harris was the radio-telephone operator—RTO—for 1st Platoon's Sergeant Hugh Sutterfield. Harris was also paying attention to the Easter service but from a distance. The eighteen-year-old had never witnessed a chaplain sent into the field to minister to the troops, so he thought the exercise worthy of his attention. "...I didn't spend a lot of time thinking about God. This was an unusual event, though, and I watched out of curiosity." Besides, Harris had "...never seen soldiers in the boonies grouped so close together out in the open."[5]

What happened next was witnessed by Fisher, Marchetti, Harris, and many other Charlie Company troops, though Fisher's story was significantly different from the other two soldiers' versions. Fisher, writing five years after the fact, recalled that a listening post radioed in to report three Vietnamese armed with rifles were heading across the far side of the clearing.* Then the company commander, Captain William R. Nolen, radioed headquarters to check if any friendly units were in the area. The answer over the radio was "[n]egative, Charlie 6, they must be VC reconnaissance. Don't let them get away. We don't want your position given away." Fisher watched as the company was ordered on line parallel to the trees. Then the troopers waited for the enemy to draw closer.[6]

Harris's account was more straightforward; the Chaplain finished his service, looked out toward the clearing, pointed, and then yelled. Out there were three Vietnamese—Vietcong, Victor Charles, Mr. Charles, Charlie, Chucky—walking unawares toward the company's perimeter. The GIs sprang into action. "Within seconds several rifles were being fired."[7] No orders, no radio calls to HQ, no troopers drawn up onto a firing line. Just a turkey shoot.

"It was all an impulse thing," Pfc Phil Hall of 2nd Platoon would relate years later. "The guys had enough common sense to come on line, but there were no orders." Men were spraying the clearing with M16 rounds, pumping M79 grenades toward the Vietcong. Hall himself grabbed a "pig" (M60 machine gun) as his platoon charged across that clearing to blast away at the Vietnamese who were still a good four or five hundred meters away. Even a soldier from First Platoon left his position on the perimeter to pump a few rounds at the VC scouts.

One guerilla went down while another staggered amid the hail of bullets and explosions. Surprisingly, the third man darted toward the far trees without signs of being hit. The second VC, the staggering guerilla, toppled to the ground as more bullets chewed into him. The third man disappeared into the trees. One of the downed men made it to his feet again, only to crumple to the ground as the Americans continued to fire at him. For the charging 2nd Platoon, which provided the bulk of the fusillade, there was no covering fire or tactical advance. Instead, there was a pell-mell dash that more closely resembled a foot race at a Fourth of July picnic, replete with fireworks, than a military advance. 2nd Platoon members reached the enemy before any other soldiers.

Energized by the action, the 2nd Platoon's lieutenant, John W. Libs, was one of the first men to reach the VC bodies. The lieutenant found one of the men already dead. The other guerilla had one leg torn away below the knee, along with several bullet holes in his torso. Yet, Libs found that the second VC was not yet dead.

"Hey, Doc!" Libs called back to the medic, Fisher, who had not moved from the perimeter. "Come on up here; maybe we can use you."

Libs looked down into the dying man's face. "Where's D-800?" the excited lieutenant asked. D800 was the VC main force battalion known to be operating in the area.

Though mangled and dying, the enemy soldier managed to spit on Libs. He retaliated by seizing the dying soldier's testicles and squeezing them until the man blurted out something in Vietnamese. Libs looked to his interpreter, a member of the South Vietnamese National Police attached to the company, for an explanation.

"He's from an independent unit and was out on patrol," the interpreter answered.[8]

Fisher reached the scene of the carnage. By that time, both enemy soldiers were dead. The ghastly wounds on the bodies caused Fisher to retch. Before the new medic thought about what he was saying, measured his words, Fisher asked Sergeant Lawson Passmore why the company had not waited for the three men to walk into the unit's perimeter so the GIs could capture them instead of killing them. Perhaps it was because Fisher was the platoon's medic, responsible for keeping the wounded alive, and so a good man to be kind to, or maybe it was because Fisher was new and so not indoctrinated in the ways of war, but Passmore patiently answered the medic.

"First of all, Doc," Passmore responded in his Georgia growl, "if they had gotten close enough for us to attempt a capture they would also have been close enough to try and kill us. Would you like someone to explain to your girlfriend or your parents why you died here when it could easily have been prevented? Besides that, if we had captured them we would have no more information than we have now. The papers that they are carrying tell us all we need to know."

The Georgian finished his rationale by explaining, "[l]ast and most important, if they did survive, they would stand a good chance of defecting to our side, if only long enough to get back to their unit. One thing's for sure, Doc, the VC that I get in my sights today will not be the one who shoots me from a treetop next month."[9]

1st Platoon leader 2nd Lieutenant Smith DeVoe recalled seeing documents identifying the dead as belonging to D800, but Libs saw no incriminating papers on the dead Vietcong. However, the interpreter's explanation for where the three guerillas had come from rang false to Libs.± Libs was skeptical after a soldier who spoke a bit of Vietnamese approached the Lieutenant with a claim that the dying enemy had been more specific about what unit he was attached to than the interpreter had let on.

"I know for sure, sir, that he [the GI pointed at the dead guerilla] said he was from D800 and was sent out to find us."[10] In fact, according to the 5th Vietcong Division's official history as related in the book *Grab Their Belts to Fight them* by Warren Wilkins, two battalions from the 274th Vietcong Regiment were in the vicinity.[11]

Men from other platoons reached the scene. RTO Roger Harris had grabbed his radio and headed out to the bodies. "Before we got there Sgt. [Jimmy] Robinson had already cut off the [the corpses'] ears." Robinson explained to his platoon sergeant "...that the ears were confirmed body count and would affect the morale of the VC."[12] Others complained about Robinson's behavior, yet the trophy-taking was in keeping with Robinson's actions in the bush. Robinson was a former Marine who had joined the company in October of '65 after volunteering for a line unit because his security duty in Saigon was too tame. When he joined C, he had told the company commander, "I'm going to win the Medal of Honor." In camp, Robinson would prove to be mild-mannered, a quiet man who read and kept his carousing under control. However, in the field, the sergeant was always gung-ho, always running, and always eager to fight or claim a trophy.**

Harris also noticed that the officers were having a serious discussion concerning their present positions. Harris heard the officers discuss the possibility that the company's position was compromised because one of the VC had escaped. "It sure made things exciting," Harris recalled. "There was talk that we might have an attack on our positions that night."

The company Executive Officer (XO), Lieutenant Kenneth Alderson, felt that 2nd Platoon's actions had been unprofessional. He felt that those troopers had reacted so recklessly, bolting up and charging at the mere sight of the three Vietcong, that the company had flubbed an opportunity to capture the enemy soldiers. To Alderson's way of thinking, the one escaped guerilla had undoubtedly estimated the company's size and position and reported that information to an enemy commander. The helter-skelter charge had been shoddy work that would force the Americans to change positions.

Lieutenant Libs added a warning to the conversation, revealing what the 2nd Platoon rifleman had told him regarding the enemy unit's identity. For the company's safety, Libs urged Captain Nolen to move the unit to the far side of the clearing while also setting out an ambush for any enemy sent to retrieve the bodies.[13]

Nolan listened to Libs. The captain was a profoundly religious man who, in the short time he had been with the company, had made it clear he was more interested in God than glory. Nolan was cautious, overly cautious, choosing his every word gingerly, making decisions carefully yet projecting no conviction behind those decisions. Some company officers felt that Nolan was simply in over his head. The officers instinctively measured Nolan against the company's past commanders—the likable and professional Captain Canady and the gung-ho Captain Padilla—and the judgments did not come out in Nolan's favor. He inspired a certain respect for his religiosity, but he scored low on the combat-savvy scale. Even the battalion commander, Lieutenant Colonel William S.

Hathaway, had felt the necessity of instructing Nolan to pay special heed to Alderson's and Libs' suggestions since the officers had been in-country for so long. Libs had seen more combat than the other platoon leaders.‡ Libs projected the air of a combat-tested officer, so much so that he came off as cocky. Libs was self-professed cocky. After nine months in Vietnam, Libs still projected that picture of a warrior, but the responsibility of keeping men alive weighed on him. He geared his reactions toward protecting his men's lives. At that point, Libs told Nolen to get the men moving because it would save lives, and the captain was reacting to do precisely that.[14]

Sergeant Pete Faberski, the NCO in charge of 1st Platoon's weapons squad, noticed tension growing in the men as the company shifted to the clearing's far side. Faberski did not share their jitters. The company's non-commissioned officers—non-coms, NCOs—were used to warnings to be careful when in the bush; officers often told the sergeants that they were going up against some hardcore unit or other. Faberski's platoon sergeant, Hugh Sutterfield, instructed the men to dig prone positions—scratch out a little place for yourself in the dirt, just in case—but Sutterfield's mood matched his weapons squad sergeant's mood; he was not worried.

Other troopers in the company were not so sanguine. In-country less than two weeks, Pfc Daniel Kirby remembers some of the GIs firing off rounds at shadows. Medic Dave Marchetti could not get over the gloom that settled over the men. Only Pfc Thomas Steele's presence buoyed Dave Marchetti's spirits. Steele was a fellow Pennsylvanian (a Philadelphia native)—in combat even that shaky connection, that thread was important. Steele simply would not let Marchetti share in the gloom. He joked with Marchetti and talked about Philadelphia as if it were down the block from Marchetti's hometown of Pittsburg.

At dusk, the company's tactical communications chief, Sergeant Charles Weyant, overheard Captain Nolen on the radio with Battalion Headquarters (HQ). From the sound of Nolen's responses, Weyant determined that Major General William DePuy, 1st Infantry Division commander, was heading to the unit. Nolan ordered someone to mark the landing zone with green smoke. When DePuy's helicopter dropped from the sky, Weyant was nearby to hear the fierce commander reemphasize to Charlie Company officers the need for caution. The dead scout seemed to verify that a large number of VC were in the vicinity. Weyant heard DePuy speak with Lieutenant Frank Fox, the artillery forward observer, about artillery support. The general finished his visit by reminding the officers that the downed VC confirmed other intelligence that D800, a main force enemy battalion, was nearby. That bit of news meant Charlie Company could expect to have their perimeter probed that night. Since Operation ABILENE's goal was to locate and eradicate the enemy, D800's proximity was a good thing.

In late March 1966, two of the First Infantry Division's three brigades had been committed to Operation ABILENE. The Big Red One—the Division was nicknamed for the distinctive red number "1" stitched on its shoulder patch—was the instrument chosen by General William Westmoreland to carry out the operation. Westmoreland, commander of American forces in Vietnam, had targeted two regiments of the PLAF (People's Liberation Armed Force–the Vietcong) operating in Phuoc Tuy Province. An Australian Army officer studying the depth of communist domination of the province pronounced that Phuoc Tuy "was an area which had gone bad...The VC were pretty much in control of it."[15] Westmoreland believed that the enemy would use Phuoc Tuy Province as a jumping-off point for a summer offensive against

Saigon. Operation ABILENE was Westmoreland's way of beating the Vietcong to the punch.[16] Fifty "Huey" helicopters were employed in the operation, shuttling from point to point in the province, and dropping soldiers into landing zones for search and destroy operations. Racing against the enemy's buildup of supplies and personnel in Phuoc Tuy and Long Thanh Provinces, Westmoreland's forces would knock the enemy off-balance, and onto the defensive, preempting the offensives. That at least was the scheme for the operation.[17]

Furthermore, Operation ABILENE was newly minted Major General William DePuy's opportunity to prove his pet theory that American bombs and American shells could bury the Vietcong's best. The general, fresh off Westmoreland's staff and elevated to command of the Big Red One, recognized in those VC main force units—the type of formations journalist Neil Sheehan had characterized as sledgehammer battalions, filled with motivated soldiers trained in ambush and lightning strikes—precisely the kind of targets that, if successfully smashed, would prove the general's theory.[18] If the soldiers of the Bloody Red One (as some of the troops derisively labeled it) could defeat the enemy's best forces, then charismatic, opinionated, aggressive General DePuy would have a professional as well as a tactical victory.

Certainly, Westmoreland expected as much from DePuy, whom Westmoreland considered both brilliant and, from their time working together in the Pentagon during the 1950s, a hard-charger, possessing "boundless energy,"[19] attributes that coincided with Westmoreland's expectations that the next phase of warfare (Westmoreland was finished playing defense, he now expected to push the war to the borders of Vietnam, away from populated areas) in Vietnam required "bold and skillful commanders."[20]

DePuy was a believer in the type of operations necessary to take the war to the enemy—search and destroy missions. He was the primary advocate of search-and-destroy tactics meant to pin the guerrillas so that American firepower could blast them.[21] DePuy believed that American military munitions could bury the enemy. "The solution in Vietnam is more bombs, more shells, more napalm..." the general had recently stated. "Until the other side cracks and gives up."[22]

To dump those loads of fiery death where they would produce the prerequisite amount of annihilation, DePuy believed in finding the enemy and piling on. While still chief of operations at MACV, he had put it more succinctly, "We are going to stomp them to death."[23] However, finding an enemy to stomp was proving to be problematic. The Vietcong were decidedly uncooperative in allowing the U.S. favored division or brigade-sized sweeps to scoop them up. Repeatedly, in early 1966, the big operations were coming up empty. The enemy was dictating the rate of contact. The guerrillas melted away when the big American units came lumbering their way. The VC waited to strike until they believed they had the advantage which was when they outnumbered the Americans or when an American unit was out of position.[24]

U.S. field officers had noticed this tendency to pick off the odd isolated unit. To take advantage of the enemy's tactic, American commanders began dangling bait for the enemy to snap at as part of the Americans' attempt to initiate contact. The Americans "broke down their units into platoon and company-size patrols to lure them [the Vietcong] into attacking. The risks were justified if the Communists took the bait because reinforcing units could then pile on."[25]

According to author Andrew Woods, writing forty years after the battle, Lieutenant Colonel William S. Hathaway was instructed to "entice" the enemy to attack his companies by isolating them from supporting positions. On March 30, 1966, the 2nd Battalion, 16th Regiment went hunting for the enemy by presenting their units as bait.[26] The battalion was airlifted into Landing Zone Norman on the Courtenay Rubber Plantation buried in the heart of the May Tao Secret Zone in the jungles between Saigon and the port of Vung Tau. The battalion was then scattered into its company components and sent out into the jungle to invite the enemy to strike. Battery A of the 1st Battalion, 7th Artillery, followed. Their mission was to atomize any enemy that might bite at a Big Red One infantry company. This pattern of search and destroy would be repeated through the early days of April: swarms of helicopters debouching troops into jungle clearings, then "sweeps" into that jungle in efforts to catch D800 and other elements of the enemy's 5th Division.[27§]

Many Company C men remained tense through the night of April 10/11. The unit was expecting a mortar attack or an enemy rush. Officers moved among their men, checking to make sure the soldiers were alert. While making his rounds, Libs met up with 30-year-old Lieutenant Marty Kroah of 3rd Platoon. The two officers were friends, and as the likelihood of battle loomed, Kroah took the opportunity to tell Libs, "Well, we're going to get the shit kicked out of us tomorrow."

Libs responded with a bit of pure Libs bravado, "But we found D800. We're going to kick ass, Marty."[28]

Other members of the company simply did not notice the tenseness surrounding them. Over in the 2nd Platoon's area Pfc Galen Summerlot, a recent replacement, did not sense that things were wound tight. He was just doing what the other, more experienced men were doing, standing guard and writing letters. Before Easter, he had written a letter to his folks back home in Indiana, reassuring them that things were indeed quiet.

"I am on guard [duty] again tonight. We take turns keeping awake and guarding. I don't [know] if I will ever see much action around here."

Nothing happened that night. The calm allowed medic Bob Fisher to mull over Sergeant Lawson Passmore's words regarding the overpowering use of force against the three scouts.

"I thought about what this man had said…I don't know what I had expected when I came to this country [South Vietnam], but this was not it. The rules [were] different. What might seem inhumane and immoral back home may be the only means of survival in this jungle. Right and wrong are moving targets."[29]

Writing of that night five years later, Fisher added, "Little did I know…that within 24 hours I would live with such fear and confusion that no precept…that I have held would remain."

---

*Gilbert Delao, another RTO, recalls receiving a radio message from the LP. Pfc Bobby Holton, also an RTO, recalls spotting the three Vietcong from his place along the tree line and "…trying to raise the other platoons on the F" (frequency), but he couldn't get through.

There was radio traffic before the shooting; whether it sparked the shooting is unclear.

± The Duty Officer's Log for April 10, 1966, entry for time 1947 reads: "The Dead VIETCONG had papers on him that identified him as being a member of D-800…."

**Pfcs John Babino and Bobby Holton of 1st Platoon confirmed that Robinson took the trophy. Holton also recalled that, before the operation began, First Sergeant Takeguchi urged the squad leaders to take trophies. "I want to see ears," he told the NCOs. Wes Carpenter recalled that one officer carried a pouch with a collection of trophy ears inside.

‡In a letter from General William DePuy to John Libs dated August 24, 1988, the general stated that Libs was the "real leader of the company as well as your platoon."

§In the same August 24, 1988, letter as above DePuy denied that the company had been bait. He further stated that he had only used units as bait one time in Vietnam, some months following Operation ABILENE.

Chapter Two: Walking Point

"The man walking point needs to think of himself as a 'hunter.' He has to know how to track. On ground too hard to leave a footprint: a broken snail slick meant someone had stepped on it. A trail of ants in disarray was a sign it had been disturbed.

A unit had to be aware they were hunters being hunted."

Charles Weyant, Charlie Company, 2/16,
"Rangers"

The next morning; the straps on Pfc Dave Burris' rucksack dug into his shoulders, irritating the sunburned flesh beneath his sweat-soaked fatigues. The baked skin on his chest, back, and shoulders were raw under the rucksack's weight of more than sixty pounds of military gear. A week and a day earlier, Burris had celebrated his 21st birthday by unloading a resupply helicopter under a tropical sun, and after removing his shirt to ease the heat the young soldier had collected a blistering sunburn for his birthday. Burris wondered if Vietnam was always going to be this uncomfortable. The G.I. had been with Sergeant Rolf Schoolman's squad, 3rd Platoon, for just over a month. In that time, he had lost twenty pounds to South Vietnam's heat.

Burris was walking point, lead man through a double canopy jungle near the village of Xa Cam My on the Courtenay Rubber Plantation. Walking point was a responsibility that concerned the trooper. He could not see much in the perpetual dusk of the canopy's shadows, yet he was accountable for guiding the unit safely through those shadows.

Walking point meant he was the bloodhound, the early warning, the bait, the savior, and the company's sacrificial lamb. At approximately 9:30 AM, the company had come across some empty trenches, though the fact that no Vietcong were skulking about only added to the men's sense of dread. For Burris, it was proof he was in enemy-controlled territory. He had heard that the company—all of the 2nd Battalion, 16th Regiment—was searching for a V.C. battalion, but he only had a vague feel for what he was searching for or how he was supposed to find it.

This was Burris' first day on point.

"Scared shitless" because of his new duty, Burris took comfort in the professional manner in which the squad moved behind him. A poster boy for California youth, surfer-boy blond, and a hot rod enthusiast, he was proud of the stealth the squad practiced while moving through the surprisingly dry and open landscape. Burris could find room to maneuver beneath the towering trees – as the company had moved into the towering trees' shelter that morning, the undergrowth had given way to dry green-brown ground. The heat, held down low by the canopy, clung to Burris as he picked his way through the shadows. Burris counted the squad as the platoon's best at movement through the bush. The Californian also took comfort in knowing that besides his squad stretched out behind him, the two remaining squads from the 3rd Platoon were on his right, each squad moving in a separate column through the foliage. Despite the easy mistakes that a boot on dried vegetation invited, he noted that the entire company remained silent, 4th Platoon following in three columns behind 3rd Platoon, with 1st Platoon behind 4th Platoon and 2nd Platoon on drag.* The experienced soldiers walking in those columns had marched in this area at various times in the preceding months, but for Burris, it was new. For Burris, this world of towering trees, vines, and fat-downed logs was Vietnam.

He was in an alien world. A frightening world where this day, April 11, 1966, Burris was walking point, probing for the enemy. He was destined to find them. Or more ominously, the enemy was determined to be found.

..

Operation ABILENE was a search-and-destroy mission rife with lethal contact initiated by the Vietcong.[30] Just the day before, a squad from Alpha Company had walked into a hornet's nest. During the kind of terror-filled flash fight that the enemy was expert at conducting, V.C. had ambushed a Company A squad, scything through the soldiers with machine gun and small arms fire. Then the enemy was gone, leaving one American dead and the platoon leader severely wounded.

Some members of Company C had listened to the fight over the radio. But that was another unit, other lives, another world. A more immediate cause for apprehension in the company's world had been their encounter on Easter. Three Vietcong spotted and cut down, an eye-opener for the entire company.[31]

The next day, Monday, the officers of Charlie Company were expecting a fight. Burris knew the officers and noncoms had identified the three V.C. as scouts for D800, a main force battalion and Burris also knew that the scout who got away had surely informed the enemy of the Americans' whereabouts.[32±]

That morning the 3rd Platoon leader—Dave Burris' commander—1st Lieutenant Martin Kroah was worried. A dark feeling settled over him as the company commander ordered the 3rd Platoon to take point. Kroah's Platoon had walked point many times before, but this morning it felt different, not routine, not right.

Kroah's men, or more precisely the men of Burris' squad, were each carrying more than four hundred rounds of ammunition–more than the other men of the company—to react to whatever walking point would throw at them. Sergeant Rolf Schoolman, Burris' squad leader, was a careful soldier bent on not losing a man because his squad lacked ammo during a firefight. Schoolman, whose speech carried the steely flavor of a German-naturalized American, trusted his men to fight well because he had instructed them well; he would not allow a new man's inexperience to threaten the lives of other squad members, not if he could mitigate that threat with some attention. The sergeant also knew, however, that his soldiers had to have the material to fight. And he knew that G.I.s had to be ordered to carry it. He would not leave it to tired, hot, scared men to decide what equipment to hump. Schoolman made that decision for them.

..

At the company's tail end, Specialist 4 (Spec 4) Steve Antal was pulling drag. He was the rear guard, a flanker for the three columns' left column moving northwesterly through the jungle. And he had been warned by Lieutenant Libs that there was an eighty percent chance that the company would bump into the enemy. That was not comforting information to the young Antal.

Directly in front of Antal, another flanker, Pfc Leroy Lark, was concerned not with the enemy's threat as much as the threat from his unit's leadership. The rifleman had no confidence in Captain Nolen.

Lark could not shake the dread he had felt for two days, a fear springing from the hours before the company had stopped in that clearing to await the chaplain and Easter services. To get to that clearing, Nolen had directed the company down a jungle trail that (from all signs) had seen frequent use by the Vietcong, recent use. Lark was sure about one thing—American soldiers did not use trails, not if they wanted to live. Lark knew many of the men felt the same way—this new commander, Nolen, could get a guy killed.**

Farther up the stretched-out company, at the center of the long columns, Pfc F. David Peters of the headquarters contingent was unaware that some of his fellow troopers were less than thrilled with Nolen's skills as a commander. Peters was too new to the company to judge Nolen's skills. Peters had been with the unit for one week that Monday morning. Assigned to Nolen as his temporary radio operator, Peters had observed the captain for a few days, and Nolen seemed OK to this Pfc. Yet Peters had no experience against which to judge Nolen's performance.

On that morning, Peters was still trying to get acclimatized to being the Old Man's radio operator—company commanders were invariably labeled the "Old Man" regardless of age. Captain Nolen was approximately twenty-eight at the time of Operation ABILENE. A week earlier, back at the 90th Replacement Depot Peters and other C Company replacements were called over to a helicopter to transport them to the company which was already humping the bush. A sergeant waiting next to the chopper barked out, "[A]nyone here know how to work a radio?" Peters stuck to the old bromide, "Never volunteer." The other replacements did the same. The sergeant asked again, a little louder this time. Silence. The NCO bellowed the same question a third time. No one answered. "So he looks at me [Peters] and says, 'You're the Old Man's new radio operator.'"

..

Back at point, Pfc Burris continued his careful advance while stealing looks at Sergeant Schoolman, who was five yards back, deftly guiding the young Pfc with hand signals. Despite his assignment, Burris could not help but contemplate his lot within the squad. The Pfc felt he had been accepted by the squad, emerging from his time as a nameless replacement into a bona fide platoon member.

He had even acquired a nickname, "Boots." Sergeant Schoolman had stuck Burris with the name when Burris had walked into the mess tent back at base camp wearing only his skivvies and a pair of boots. It was the Californian's effort to fight the heat. That had been his second week in Vietnam.

Sometime after Schoolman had christened him, other members of Burris' squad began acknowledging him. Burris had enjoyed the thaw. He liked to hear Pfc John "Ollie" Lang explain how he had ended up in Vietnam. "I was stationed in Berlin. Chicken shit duty. One night a load of us got drunk and returned to the barracks at 3 in the morning. Someone pounded on the captain's door, and when he answered the door, the guy told him he 'ran a chicken shit outfit. We all want to go to Vietnam!' Thirty-one days later, that's where we were."

Sergeant Richard Garner would lay out his life story in a smooth Southern drawl that Burris found almost exotic. Burris listened to the yarns but thought more about how Garner had taken him under his wing, instructing Burris on how to break down and reassemble an M16, which Burris had no experience with until he was airborne in his first helicopter ride, heading for a hot landing zone. That had been his first week with the company. Garner was just a couple of years older than Burris, but those years seemed critical to the Californian.

Then there was Randall Prinz—"Peanuts." Peanuts was an old hand, almost nine months in Vietnam, having deployed with the company when the 2nd Brigade became the vanguard of the Big Red One, shipping out in June 1965. Peanuts was a small guy and, at eighteen, younger even than Burris. The young Californian liked and respected his fellow Pfc. Peanuts shared Burris' love of fast cars. Peanuts had exuberantly shared visions of the "cherry screamer" he was going to "soup up" when his tour of duty was finished. Peanuts and Burris had a meeting of the minds in agreeing that a Dodge or Plymouth "Hemi" was *the machine*. Peanuts would talk with everyone about cars. One GI, Richard Jenkins of California, who was already stateside because of wounds sustained before the battle of Xa Cam My, reflected on Prinz and his love of automobiles.

"He and I had about the same interests. He had a 1956 Dodge" Jenkins recalled. "He got it from his Mom and Dad. A hand-me-down car. He thought it was about the hottest piece of iron they had built in Detroit."

At 18 Peanuts didn't really have a lot of experience with cars, but he liked to talk about them, and Jenkins was happy to oblige. When the brigade was shipping over in 1965 the two had spent the time aboard the ship talking cars or reminiscing about the "good old days" in their respective hometowns. Peanuts became a friend, and as their time in-country wore on, the Midwesterner became like a younger brother to Jenkins. Prinz was so likable that Jenkins encouraged the kid from Roseville, Michigan to correspond with his younger sister Carol. The two soldiers made plans for Peanuts to visit California when they made it out of Vietnam. That changed when Jenkins had been wounded and sent home. Still, Peanuts remained, and Burris took up where Jenkins had left off. The new Californian took just as much of a liking to Peanuts as the old Californian had done. Burris just did not have a sister to promise to Prinz.

..

Burris's self-assessment went on until 11:00 AM when Sergeant Schoolman signaled Burris to halt. Schoolman moved up and pointed Burris due west. The sergeant whispered, "If you want to see that wife and little baby again, watch what you're doing." Burris had been bragging to some of the guys that his wife had a baby on the way.

Minutes after the shift in direction, as the company was moving through a tangled patch that limited visibility to no more than twenty feet, another of Kroah's squads discovered a trail. The company stopped while Captain Nolen ordered patrols out to reconnoiter.[33]

The 3rd Platoon sergeant, Everett Eugene Langston—known affectionately as the "Round Man"—drifted back toward the middle of the company to locate 1st Platoon's Sergeant Hugh Sutterfield. The two sergeants, friends and fellow Arkansans, took advantage of the respite to hold an impromptu war conference. The noncoms' practiced eyes told them that the trail was dangerous. The Round Man noted that the old hands were tired and careless from being too long in the field, while the replacements were too green to sense the danger. Sutterfield may have commented that the new company commander was pushing ahead regardless of the enemy signs along the trail. Other than a few nervous grunts who overheard the conversation, the NCOs kept their worries to themselves. However, before Langston had shown, Sutterfield had voiced the same concerns to Pete Faberski, his weapons squad sergeant.

Faberski and Sutterfield were both "short" – their tours of duty in Vietnam were almost over; each had approximately sixty days remaining in Vietnam.

The trail located by Langston's 3rd Platoon had the look of recent use by a large number of men. That was bad news. Neither Faberski nor Sutterfield wanted to see a green captain walk them into a trap.

Sadness seemed to perpetually hover around Faberski; sadness, uncertainty, even in the best of circumstances. One Charlie Company soldier observed, "Pete had that 'little boy lost' look." Of average height, with a slight build, and a swath of black hair on his head, it was the sorrow ever-present in the sergeant's eyes that stayed with many who met him.

Faberski was no coward struggling with fear for his well-being. Though self-preservation was a part of his apprehension for the future, the sergeant's concern had more to do with his Second Platoon men, than fear of getting his ass shot off. Faberski's apprehension grew out of his own experience of war. He knew war as something more vivid/dirty/

horrifying/permanent than the glorious dyings of an ersatz-soldier John Wayne envisioned by the naïve youths of his platoon. It was that reality of war that darkened the sergeant's eyes, molding them into pockets of sorrow. In war, men die. Faberski knew that some of these young men raised on John Wayne soldiering, Randolph Scott heroics, and Errol Flynn secret missions, would die.

Faberski lived with childhood memories of Berlin under a rain of allied bombs. In 1945, as a seven-year-old, Faberski had witnessed the battered city crumble in a blistering Götterdämmerung. Bodies, black bloody bodies, had littered the streets of his Friedenau district neighborhood – bodies not of Hitler's Supermen killed defending the Fatherland from the Red hordes, but rather, the bodies of neighbor women young Pete knew; mothers who had braved Russian rockets and cannons to search the Berlin rubble for water and food to feed their children.

Young Pete had lived weeks in a rank cellar beneath the bombed-out home of a dead family friend. He had known only fear and hunger for months. Fear of the enemy, fear of starvation. He feared the monster Russians who raped and looted, taking those valuables still left a prostrate people. After the killing stopped, he feared the "hunger typhoid," a virulent disease killing the old and the young of the city. He feared that he might never see his soldier father or his soldier brother again. He feared in an inchoate, primitive way what his father and brother might have become.

It would be a year before his father returned from a British POW camp. The brother, a seventeen-year-old boy promoted to werewolf when dragooned into the Wehrmacht in '45, never returned.

Faberski knew war.

..

After Langston headed back to his platoon, Sutterfield determined that he had to warn the captain about the dangerous path, literally dangerous path, that the officer was heading down. Pfc Roger Harris, Sutterfield's RTO, followed along as the ageless noncom – Sutterfield, a World War II veteran who was as trim as the kids he commanded, "stomped through the jungle to Captain Nolen's position."[34] If Nolen saw Sutterfield coming the officer would have noticed Sutterfield's "odd little smile" and the clear gray stare that commanded Nolen's attention. Sutterfield did not raise his voice, but rather, in an even flat tone that garnered absolute attention, he told Nolen to "wake the hell up and realize what you're doing." Sutterfield then shut up and let his massive stare pile up on top of his extended silence to make his point.

..

Sixty-four men had joined the company since March 1st.[35] One of these, Pfc Mark Ferrell, died before April 11. Mark had been riding in a two-and-a-half-ton truck—a deuce-and-a-half—on his first day in-country and rested his chin on the muzzle of his loaded M16 as the truck jolted down the road. The transport hit a bump, the M16 discharged, and Mark's head was blown off. A stupid mistake. With Mark's death, sixty-three replacements were left to fill Charlie Company's ranks. Fifty-two of these men had been in Vietnam a month or less on the morning of April 11th, 1966.[36] In the seasoned soldiers' parlance, these new G.I.s were "cherry/newfer/new meat/fenugie/greenseed/twink," or FNGs: Fucking New Guys. For the most part, these new soldiers were ignored by the "old hands"—those soldiers who had been in-country for some time—because "new meat" could get a G.I. killed by doing something seriously stupid.[37] 135 Charlie Company troops were trekking through the jungles near Xa Cam My on April

11, of whom sixty-three were these new troops. That's a lot of room for stupid mistakes.

..

One such mistake had come a few months earlier from an unlikely new guy. Sergeant Parks (not his real name) joining the company was a good thing. He was a crack shot, a marksman from the Army's competition rifle team. He was also an old friend of Sergeant Sutterfield's, who had also been on the rifle team back in the states. Sutterfield's OK made Parks all right. The fucker would introduce the company to the reality of friendly fire.

Parks replaced someone in the third Squad, 1st platoon, but he came and went so quickly that it was fuzzy regarding which soldier he replaced and what his function in the company was supposed to be. Men were reaching the end of their hitch, had to be replaced and well, hell, the company could do worse than getting a member of the Army's rifle team. Parks brought along his rifle as well, his special target shooting M14.

Only 1st Squad's sergeant, Barnicoat had a problem with Parks. To Barnicoat's thinking, all that shooting—those years of greasing paper targets and zapping clay pigeons and zeroing in on tree limbs and blowing apart mounds of dirt—had done wonders for Park's eyesight, but nothing for his hearing, which had been pulverized. Son-of-a-bitch couldn't hear shit out of one ear. When it looked like Parks was going to land in 1st Squad, Barnicoat complained to a superior. Parks was shifted to 3rd squad. There was never a question about ridding the company of him—already the manpower shortages that would hamstring American combat troops all their years in Vietnam were showing up in Charlie Company.

This had been in early November of 1965 and Parks would only last a few days.

Particular Bravery: The Battle of Xa Cam My And The Death of a Grunt Company

As darkness descended on the night of November 12, 1965, the men of Company C relaxed. The company had set up its perimeter in a safe area, fairly safe area, and no one was expecting trouble that night. That is, no one who had been in-country any length of time and had acquired some combat savvy. Parks had been in-country only days, and the only savvy he displayed was in the way he handled his rifle.

PFC Franklin Conn, 3rd Squad, and PFC Gary Whitley, 1st squad were sent out on LP (Listening Post). They were fifty yards (or 150 yards, or ten miles—depending on whom you talk to) in front of the perimeter, fifty yards to the front of a skittish Parks. When the moon came up Conn and Whitley yelled back to the perimeter that they were moving, just like they were supposed to do—not letting the sleepy men on the perimeter know you were moving could get you shot in Vietnam. Parks, who wasn't sleepy but who couldn't hear a bulldozer in a library, challenged the two moving figures to his front. Of course, he couldn't hear their response and he whipped that rifle up to his shoulder and fired.

Two shots licked out of the perimeter. Two shots, two hits. That son-of-a-bitch Parks sure could shoot. Couldn't hear worth a damn, but he could shoot. Didn't matter whether it was dark or not, he hit both shadows way out in front of him; hit chubby, affably, only-child Conn in the chest, and caught Whitley in the leg.

The perimeter roared awake. Dog-tired soldiers were instantly alert, clutching rifles, straining to make sense of the shouting coming from the darkness. The shouting was actually screaming. "Medic, Medic. We've been hit. We've been hit." Men were scrambling in the dark; low along the ground, keeping their heads down in case this was an assault.

Sergeant Faberski could hear someone saying, "it's friendly fire." He knew he had to get out to the wounded. He crawled it to the LP, the first one there. He saw Conn laid out on the ground, blood spurting from a chest wound. Conn gurgled something to Faberski. The sergeant couldn't understand the words, so he reflexively said, "Don't worry Conn, you're going to make it. You're going to be all right."

Conn responded, "You think so sarge? Are you sure?" His eyes were full of hope for just a moment, those automatic words from Faberski bringing Conn a moment of peace as he bled to death.

A medic showed up. He gave Conn a quick look and told Faberski he was gone. The medic moved to Whitley. He shouted at Faberski, who was frozen over Conn's corpse, "This guy we can help. This guy can make it."

Faberski stalked back to where a distraught Parks was being questioned by Sutterfield and others. "You stupid bastard," Faberski screamed. Sutterfield was holding Parks' rifle. Parks was crying.

Away went Whitley to a field hospital and eventually to the US.

Away went Conn's body, transported unceremoniously on the back of a jeep driven by Klaus Grill. "Captain Canady didn't want him [Conn's body] around in the morning when everyone woke up." Grill explained.

"It was dark, the jeep had a big radio in the back, no seat. I wrapped him [Conn's body] up in a poncho and laid him over that radio. I was going to take him to battalion medic. It's dark and I'm going out there all alone, weren't really roads out there. This guy [Conn's body] kept falling off. I'd take a turn and he'd fall off. I'd stop and put him back on [the jeep]. Pretty soon I started laughing and talking to him.

'Listen Sonabitch, stay put.'

It wasn't funny that he was killed, but he kept falling off. Finally, I just had to grip him with one hand and drive with the other to make it [to battalion HQ]."

Away went Sergeant master-shooter, good-friends-with-Sutterfield Parks. Parks was broken by the incident, a nervous wreck, and certainly, the men didn't want him around any longer. He was transferred to Saigon. Someone down there put him in charge of shipments at Tan Sun Nhut. No one from the company remembers if he took his rifle with him when he left.

New guys could get you killed or sometimes, they could kill you.

..

On top of the likelihood of mistakes from replacements was the old hands' loss of combat effectiveness. General Westmoreland believed that Phase Two, the phase that Americans were engaged in during the spring of 1966, of his three-phased war required that U.S. troops aggressively patrol the countryside, forcing the enemy to show its face. Westmoreland was sending American troops into enemy base areas that had hitherto been untouchable.[38] This offensive strategy meant that C Company soldiers had been so persistently "humping the boonies" in the opening months of 1966 that many of the old hands were sporting ripped and tattered clothing from the effects of razor-edged elephant grass and humidity, while their morale and reflexes were bogged down by dulled senses and tired bodies. One trooper recalled that "everyone was tired and slow…too many days in the bush without a break. We were done in." Another GI, Sergeant Harold Hunter of 4th Platoon, said, "There were guys in the unit who would sacrifice carrying ammo to carry extra food. It was part of old-timers becoming lax."

According to Sergeant Pete Faberski and Pfc Roger Harris, both of 1st Platoon, many of the old hands were eyeing their DEROs date two months out much harder than they were watching the jungle. Some twenty-five or more of the company's soldiers picking through the jungle that morning had been part of the original contingent of Charlie Company (like Faberski and Sutterfield) that had deployed from Ft. Riley, Kansas, to South Vietnam in June 1965. Another healthy handful (like Sergeant Rolf Schoolman and Pfc John Noyce) had been sent over in the months immediately following the deployment. These men had reached the stage in their tours when they began believing that they could survive Vietnam with some luck and caution. Such a belief dulled aggressiveness. The jungle veterans had not grown careless; they had grown too careful. Being too careful, combined with the old hands' general weariness and the new men's pure greenness, meant that Sergeant Sutterfield was convinced that he had to protect the company. Upon seeing the condition of the trail Sutterfield had to warn Captain Nolen, "Hey, we're heading for trouble. You may not have realized it yet, but we are."‡

..

Trails and roads that were not booby-trapped or well-traveled could still be dangerous or appear to be so. In September of '65, during a company-sized sweep in the area of Phu Cuong, the unit had performed a night move to an area that contained a leper colony. One of the platoons included Sutterfield's 1st Platoon. The event that transpired rapidly passed into Charlie Company legend, and there seemed to be as many versions of the story as there were men on the road that night – or men who later heard about it. Yet all the witnesses and all the hearsay agreed on the major point, it was only in the nuances of the story that company men differed. PFC Dave Stewart's account is a good place to start the tale, "Two platoons were single file on one side of the road and two on the other; we had been on the march since…morning. Up ahead we could see a village and word was passed down our side of the road that a leper colony was up ahead." As word spread of the lepers, one soldier across the road from Stewart unshouldered his rifle and went all jittery.

Sergeant Charles Barnicoat of 1st squad picks up the story there. "We were someplace in the middle of the column. The column stopped. we heard whispering, mumble, mumble, until it came back to us. [Sam] Bragg gets the word and turned around to me and with deadly seriousness says, 'Sarge, there's a leprechaun on the road!'"

Vietnam didn't have enough yellow demons for Sam Bragg, it now how little green men out to zap him as well. Barnicoat assured the Pfc that no leprechauns were gunning for Charlie Company, but Bragg stayed hinked up until the unit made it back to base. Then he had to live with the good-natured ribbing that followed him through the remainder of his tour. The enemy had allies in Vietnam, and they weren't just the Communist Chinese!

The story stuck to Bragg and the company. The story had staying power because it was a release valve, a way for the soldiers of C to laugh at the danger on the trails while pawning off their fear of the hostile weirdness onto a single man among them. Bragg had unwittingly expressed a collective fear of the insanity, and demonstrated the collective futility of defense, in the macabre world of humping the boonies in Vietnam. These soldiers embraced the misunderstanding because they knew that misunderstanding a word, or a deed, could get you killed on a trail. Luckily, in Bragg's case, the misunderstanding only garnered a laugh. The riflemen could use the story to isolate their lurking skittishness; make a joke of it, because the event, or, the story growing out of the event, seemed to say that the worst that could happen in Vietnam was to be hunted in a jungle by stealthy little Irish men hiding their pot of gold along a jungle trail. As Sutterfield warned the company commander on that April day of the dangers along the trail, the story of Bragg's fright was less funny as instead, it seemed to highlight the dangers of jungle trails and all the threats those paths could present.

..

Nolen had to wrestle with pressures other than a career noncom's gut feelings about the trails – or perhaps Nolen was too new to the unit to have heard the story of the leprechaun. The story probably would not have mattered even if he knew it—the captain had been urged westward. In his book *Mud Soldiers*, George Wilson writes, "[General] DePuy had left no doubt he wanted to find and smash D800."[39] Lieutenant Kroah thought it unclear whether this urging from higher up was a martial nudge to find D800 or instead a prompting to reach an extraction point. Sergeant Sutterfield may have wanted to warn the captain that the company was indeed in harm's way, but objectively, putting the company in harm's way and so drawing out the enemy was what DePuy intended. Nolen had done nothing wrong; he had not made any bad decisions. Though many company soldiers felt something big was about to pop, at that time Nolen had encountered nothing that was out of the ordinary. Although the other companies involved in Operation ABILENE had come across trails that morning, and snipers had been harassing troopers throughout ABILENE, there was nothing more than a business-as-usual morning and a sergeant's gut feelings to react to.[40] When the reconnoitering patrols failed to flush out any enemy, Nolen ordered the columns forward.

At the front of the company, Kroah knew better than to hike the trail. He ordered the men forward, paralleling the enemy track. Patrols, acting as flankers, were sent out through the green maze to keep tabs on the trail.

..

Burris was careful but he had relaxed. It was hot. The company was expecting contact with the enemy, yet the private was self-congratulatory for "conducting himself pretty well" on his first time on point. Alone at the sharp end of the mighty weapon that was a combat-ready United States Army division, some of Burris' feelings of well-being—besides the relief at not making a mistake—could be chalked up to the miles and piles of supplies, munitions, and personnel lined up in his mind's eye to come to his assistance, should he need such help.

A flash through the shadows sent him flopping to the ground. Behind him, Sergeant Schoolman dropped.

"What's going on?"

"Saw something. I think I saw someone." Burris answered, his gaze locked on the gloom before him. Schoolman inched forward. Together, weapons ready, the sergeant and the private edged forward. Five, ten yards. Nothing out there but more jungle.

"Stay alert," Schoolman told Burris and waved the column forward.

Schoolman had confidence in Burris. An event, a minor thing, from the morning had convinced Schoolman that Burris was a good man on point. As the morning began, the company awaited the resupply helicopter and the evacuation of a sergeant who had sprained his ankle; Lieutenant Kroah had detailed Schoolman's squad to do a short reconnaissance in the direction of the day's geographic objective, identified as Phase Line Blue. Schoolman had chosen Burris for point, a test for the Pfc.

Schoolman had an eye for a soldier's potential and a knack for drawing out that potential and utilizing it for the squad and platoon's benefit. The sergeant's common sense and combat instincts had won his squad's confidence. He had discovered what each squad member could do well and, whenever possible had them perform those duties. Schoolman used Randall "Peanuts" Prinz as a grenadier, an M79 man because the kid was a dead shot with the grenade launcher. The sergeant relied on Sergeant Ronald Seasholtz as a fire team leader; Seasholtz showed a maturity that Schoolman trusted, plus Seasholtz knew how to talk to his troops in a way that kept them calm even in tight situations. Schoolman had even found a use for Spec 4 Carl Klopfer, the World War II vet who seemed a bit slow. Schoolman had made the G.I. a kind of walking supply post, carrying extras for the squad: extra socks, rations, razors—a commissary in combat boots. With the quick run out on the morning of April 11, Schoolman had tested his hunch that Burris would make a good point man.

The patrol had proven uneventful: no trails, no V.C. Then, as Schoolman motioned for Burris to head back to the company perimeter, the Pfc had caught sight of something. The G.I. hit the ground, and like dominos toppling after the fall of a single piece, the squad went to ground. Burris checked out where the "something" had been; he reported to Schoolman that a large bird was scrambling through the underbrush. The squad rose and dusted themselves off—the remainder of the patrol passed without incident. Schoolman liked what he had seen of Burris' work on point. The kid was careful, the bird incident proved that, and Schoolman wanted careful out front.

Burris had not been so sure after the short reconnaissance; once back in the perimeter, preparing to begin the day's business, he could not seem to "get my act together." The quick patrol, on point, and that bird, had rattled him. In frustration,

Burris looked at Schoolman, "This just isn't going to be my day." Schoolman snapped back, "Don't say that, it's bad luck." Now, as the company moved forward, those words hung in the air.

At noon the company broke for lunch. Kroah ordered Schoolman to place a listening post forward of the company's position, and again Schoolman chose to put Burris out front. The sergeant positioned the Pfc fifteen yards ahead of the squad, a .30 caliber machine gun crew approximately ten yards behind him.

Burris noted that the land fell off northwestward. He finished his C rations while scanning the ground. Quiet; spooky quiet. No peeping birds, no sound. Nothing before him but the ground sloping off gradually, vines hanging from the trees, anthills, and a man moving out of the noon shadows – a man clad in a white shirt, shorts, and pith helmet. With his M16, Burris drew a bead on the approaching stranger, who was bent at the waist. The stranger, twenty-five yards away, had not spotted him. Burris turned back toward the .30 crew to get their attention. They were busy talking in hushed tones or eating or just skylarking; they did not see Burris' hand motions or hear his low hisses. Burris was alone.

The G.I. carefully, quickly, turned back toward the stranger. The man still had not seen him. Burris fired. The man stood straight up, erect like a nutcracker soldier.

"Oh, shit! Did I just shoot an innocent villager?" the thought flooded Burris' mind.

Then the stranger moved, jumping toward a tree, and Burris saw the holster on the man's hip. Burris fired again. The pith helmet toppled off. Then the stranger was gone.

"What the...what's going on?!!!" Schoolman was there instantly, running crouched at the waist.

"I just saw a gook down there."

At the company command post, Lieutenant Kroah heard the shot. He headed for the listening post. Halfway to the destination, the lieutenant met Schoolman, who was moving back through the platoon to find him. The two leaders turned around and hastened back to Burris. Kroah asked Burris what had happened.

"I saw a gook down there," Burris repeated for his lieutenant.

Kroah and Schoolman side-slipped out in front of Burris' position. They looked around and then returned to the Pfc. They studied Burris for a moment, like, "oh yeah, we got this new guy."

"Did you hit him?" Kroah asked.

"No."

"Stay alert, and make sure you get a hit next time."

Kroah, working his way back to the command post, was stopped by shouts of "they're here, they're here," and then two cracks of an M16. Kroah could not see the man firing, the shouts, and the rifle fire coming from a different column. Kroah moved off to this new wrinkle. When Kroah reached the G.I., whatever the trooper had seen was gone. Kroah remained calm, told the soldier to be alert, and notify the command post if he saw anything else. As the lieutenant walked back toward the command post, he noticed that the men were still working at their C rations—it was only 12:15 PM—fifteen minutes since the company had stopped for lunch.

Upon reaching Captain Nolen, Kroah reported, "We've got contact."[41]

Nolen ordered Kroah to get a patrol moving forward. Kroah sent a squad forward. Five minutes later, the patrol walked into a sniper's sights. One of Kroah's men went down with a round through the shoulder – Charlie Company had its first casualty of the day. Kroah again hustled to the head of his platoon. His radio operator, Jasper Conway,[§] an Alabaman with a shock of red hair, followed Kroah. Conway rattled off several shots from his M16 as he reached the locale where the trooper had been hit.

"What the hell are you shooting at?" demanded Kroah.

"I don't know how to explain it, but they just walked into the ground." Conway searched for words to identify a vanished enemy. "They were walking and then they went down."

Kroah sized up the situation. The terrain was flat; any VC the radioman may have seen must have disappeared into a bunker or tunnel. The lieutenant thought, "OK, we can deal with this."[42]

He warned Nolen over the PRC 25 radio.

"What do you think we should do?" Nolen asked.

"Find out where they're going," Kroah replied.

"That's affirm," answered Nolen.[43]

One of Kroah's men once said of him, "He didn't back up from much." He was not about to back up now. Kroah's attitude, one that helped earn him an officer's commission from the enlisted ranks, had long been, "If that idiot lieutenant can do it, I know damn well I can." He was a confident man, one who did not suffer fools gladly. Neither did he balk at danger, which was why he had not hesitated to advise Nolen on how to fight. It was advice born of his many years as an enlisted man, his many years as a "wild-assed former sergeant who knew how to fight and win."[44]

Kroah fought for Uncle Sam's Army, an Army that was also his home, a home bought at the cost of his hardscrabble youth. He joined the Army at seventeen when he decided that no one in his small Pennsylvania hometown would hire a draft-age boy destined for military service. After serving nine years as an enlisted man, he became disgusted with following the orders of an officer he deemed worthless. The officer and the orders. He volunteered for Officer Candidate School, went to Ft. Benning,

Georgia, and graduated a second lieutenant — one of the idiots. That experience, that education through the ranks, taught him how far and hard to push a commander, especially an experienced commander.

After a stint in Korea, he was assigned to the Fourth Infantry Division at Ft. Lewis, Washington. He was the executive officer for a battalion's administration company. Stir crazy after a year of mundane duties; he was eager to get away, so he volunteered for Vietnam. The move was not about career or overt patriotism; it was about a surefire way to escape the drudgery. Asking for more officer school could get turned down but asking to go to Vietnam got you an airline ticket to the Far East.

In October 1965, he arrived in Vietnam. An individual replacement, Kroah made it just in time for the end of the company's breaking-in period. 2nd Brigade embarked on Operation VIPER. It was a one-battalion "sanitizing" mission, search and destroy in the area Di Ann-Phu Loi so the division's headquarters – slated for that area – would be secure. It turned into a warm welcome for Kroah, with "several sharp battles at close quarters," as Charlie Company and the rest of the battalion clawed through heavily bunkered positions, digging out well-traveled tunnels and busting up base camps. The company lost men—some to the hard-to-take friendly fire—and G.I.s who had been in Vietnam since day one claimed that it was the most brutal fighting they had seen. Kroah handled his men well, even as he learned the ropes of combat. *"If that idiot Lieutenant can do it, I know damn well I can."*

Kroah, at thirty, was older than most of the men in the company. If not wiser, Kroah soon earned the reputation as the company hell-raiser and exercised that reputation while in base camp with an officer's prerogative but an enlisted man's abandon. An all-in fighter in the bush, the man you wanted beside you in a tight situation. Assessing the situation this April day, Kroah quickly "decided that the Vietcong were attempting to delay, or were trying to pull the company away from a Vietcong complex or base camp."[45]

No one else in the company had moved. Soldiers were still sitting, scratching at their C-rations and listening to the occasional pop of small arms fire coming from the direction of the 3rd Platoon. The more experienced G.I.s were not particularly alarmed by the fire—standard Vietcong procedure, potshots and run was how it sounded. In *Mud Soldiers*, George Wilson poses the question of whether Nolen should have called for reinforcements at that point.[46] There had been contact. The company had seen well-traveled trails, indicators that they were on the cusp of a significant encounter. Or these things could mean nothing. Nolen must have believed that these things were not events that warranted reinforcements. The company XO, Ken Alderson, wondered at Nolen's decision to sit so long in the same place while Kroah's patrols hunted for the enemy. With evidence of large numbers of VC haunting the area, Alderson believed the company should be moving so that the enemy could not develop a coordinated attack on a stationary unit. Still, Alderson felt for Nolen and understood the conflicting pressures weighing on the man. Roger Harris was also uneasy about sitting in the jungle for so long, especially after Sutterfield had warned the captain of the dangers in the area.[47] Of more immediate concern for 2nd Platoon's Medic Bob Fisher had been the red ants hanging from tree leaves along the route the company had taken through the jungle. "They [the ants] were ½ an inch long and packed a fierce bite. To walk into a nest of them unaware would be to walk away with hundreds of tiny, painful bites all over your body." Now sitting like the rest of the platoon, Fisher did not like the firing he heard toward the company's front, but he believed empathically in the company's ability to handle any situation erupting from the enemy's jungle.[48]

By 12:35, the situation changed. Pfc Milton Lader of 1st Platoon, sitting in the center of the company, recalled that when the shooting started coming from both the company's front and rear, he knew "something was up." However, at this point, the men in the middle of the company did not have a firm grasp on the precarious situation developing for Company C.

Farther back along the company's flank, Pfc Phil Hall of 2nd Platoon knew that he was in danger. He was being shot at! Lieutenant Libs had ordered Hall to move out on the platoon's left flank when the company moved parallel to the well-traveled trail. Hall worked as a flanker sitting out in the bush twenty or thirty meters from the halted platoon's position.

"I'm sitting on the ground and mumbling to myself about the predicament I'm in. I'm not real happy with where I'm at. Shots are being fired. I have a shotgun [twelve gauge] when out in front of me, I saw a squad of Vietnamese in Khaki uniforms. I didn't know who they were, I'd never seen front-line Vietcong before. Before that [April 11], it had been pretty much pajama-type guys. So I hollered that 'I got people out here in Khaki uniform.'"

That was Hall's mistake "…because no more than I hollered than I started being fired [on] from two positions." It was not the squad of Vietcong Hall had spotted that was attempting to use the American for target practice. Two other enemy infiltrators had managed to take positions close to the flanker. "One was in a tree and the other was behind a termite mound." These two guerillas hurled a torrent of small arms fire that ripped up the brush around Hall but failed to hit him. Hall hugged the ground as the two inept Vietcong missed him with their fire.

At the company's rear, Pfc Lark heard the shooting though he had yet to see the enemy. He also heard some rustling out in the scrub, and playing it safe, he sent a burst of metal down the barrel of his M16 toward movement in his front. A frantic yell, then the bleating in English came from the bushes—a 2nd Platoon G.I. had slipped into the underbrush to shit, and he had forgotten to tell anyone. Lark had shot him in the ass.

Sergeant Charles Urconis, a South Carolinian who had only been with the company a brief time, was quick to dress down Lark over the incident. Urconis practiced several select epithets on the Pfc. The sergeant ordered up the medic, Bob Fisher, who quickly ascertained that the soldier was not severely wounded because "[h]e was writhing around...moving much too fast to have been injured... seriously. When I checked him out, it was more of a grazing wound with almost no bleeding." Fisher felt that the wound was so minor that a bandage would be overkill, except that because the injury was high on the buttocks when the G.I. started walking through the jungle again, his web gear or backpack might irritate the wound.

According to Pfc Antal, Lieutenant Libs showed up to walk the wounded man up to the command contingent in the center of the columns. This unfortunate trooper (his name is lost to the record) was later reported as the 2nd Platoon's first casualty of the battle.

Lark did not have time to appreciate the upbraiding from Urconis. Moments after the trooper was escorted toward the CP, Lark spotted "four or five" uniformed guerillas attempting to "slide down our flank to see how far our unit stretched." Lark and Antal fired at the same time. Return fire was directed toward the two GIs. Lark's M16 jammed. Antal picked his shots. An enemy soldier went down. A couple of enemy grenades bounced off low branches and exploded harmlessly out in front of Lark and Antal. Lark cleared the jam and fired off six more rounds when the rifle jammed again. Luckily, the Vietcong did not press their advantage, retreating off into the jungle.

Lark cleared the M16 again, and he and Antal darted after the fleeing VC. The GIs were heading away from the company, back the way the company had come, pursuing a force of at least three enemies (Antal saw only three enemy soldiers). It was not the kind of action Lark knew his friend Pfc Eugene Garrett would have approved. Back in January, Garrett had given Lark, who was new in Vietnam at the time, some advice—avoid gathering souvenirs from villages (they could be booby-trapped) and Garrett told Lark never to go at the war gung-ho (the mission was to get home in one piece). Garrett would have been stunned to see his friend Lark and Antal rushing through the jungle like berserkers. As they moved, Lark dropped off to Antal's right and called out, "Steve, we'll have them in a crossfire."

Antal lost sight of the enemy but kept running and firing. He charged toward a rise while automatic weapons fire heated up the air around him. He hustled toward a colossal tree even as machine-gun fire traversed the area in front of him. Antal rounded the tree triggering his M16 but still resisted the temptation to switch it to automatic and blaze away. Lark appeared from off to the south, his M16 working fine as it ripped the rise that suddenly and inexplicably had become these two Americans' objective.

This firefight was over. The two Americans had stung the guerillas with their pell-mell dash, guns blazing. Antal and Lark looked at one another, did not say a word, turned back toward the company's position, and *walked* back through the jungle to the 2nd Platoon.

Yards away from Antal and Lark, Rick Owens of Louisville, Kentucky, spotted a column of uniformed VC running *toward* the three platoons further up the column. Owens did not discharge his weapon; the enemy had run past him in such a flash that he could not take deliberate aim. Owens was a believer in fire discipline, he would not fire unless he had a clear shot, which the glimpses and shadows darting by did not offer. What Owens could see from his position at the back of the company was that the enemy was unclear about where the column ended. The enemy was concentrating their fire on the three leading American platoons while leaving the 2nd Platoon unscathed, at least for the moment.

At the company commander's side, Pfc Gilbert Delao, Nolen's company RTO—newbie Pfc Dave Peters was working the battalion frequency—caught the report from 2nd Platoon, from Lark, that the guerillas were in uniform. Nolen now had what he had been pressing for; these snipers were no part-time guerrillas out to zap a few Americans—these soldiers were main force Vietcong.

And these enemy soldiers were probing the company hard. On 2nd Platoon's northern flank—on the far side of the platoon from Hall, Lark, and Antal—a fire team leader, Sergeant Robert Rexroad, had established a two-man observation post about thirty meters from the perimeter, per Lieutenant Lib's orders. At approximately the same time Hall was pinned down on the southern flank by the two snipers and Lark and Antal were busy chasing the enemy at the rear of the platoon, a khaki-clad enemy squad began working through the trees and underbrush in front of Rexroad's observation post. Rexroad's men spotted the advancing enemy and began burning up the jungle twenty meters to their front with M16 fire. The enemy pounded back at the O.P., their concentrated fire threatening to overwhelm the two Americans at the O.P. Reacting to what was happening, Rexroad sprinted from the perimeter while ripping the air with M16 rounds. The enemy directed "a hail of…fire" toward the charging Rexroad. Miraculously, he avoided being brought down. Rexroad then added his firepower to that of the observation post soldiers until the guerilla assault slackened. Rexroad then moved his men back to the perimeter.[49]

Up front in 3rd Platoon's area, the small arms fire was increasing. Nolen ordered 1st Lieutenant George Steinberg and his 4th Platoon to cover the 3rd Platoon's left flank. Steinberg, considered by the other officers as a thinker of the scattered-brained variety, instead of a fighter, "swung his platoon out from behind Kroah's men," attempting to come on line even as an enemy machine gun opened on his platoon. The .51 caliber machine gun had considerable killing power. It fired down a curtain of steel that ripped off arms and legs and blew nasty holes in human flesh. Pfc Marion Acton, 4th Platoon point man on this day, bounded forward with his M16 blazing. The .51 dropped him. The first 4th Platoon KIA for this fight. There would be more.[50]

The same burst of machine-gun fire that killed Acton also clipped Lieutenant Steinberg's arm. The miracle was that the blond lieutenant, the one officer not considered a fighter, continued fighting. As the heavy machine gun continued its deadly swing through the 4th Platoon's ranks, Staff Sergeant Bozy Gerald and Sergeant Harold Hunter hit the ground. The two African American noncoms, the two friends, were pinned down. The entire platoon was pinned down.

..

3rd Platoon's situation was sinking into the abyss as well. When Kroah had earlier prompted Nolen to find out where the enemy was located, Schoolman's squad moved forward. Burris was out front. The squad inched forward on the left; the point man spotted uniformed enemy soldiers dash from cover and as quickly disappear. Burris signaled for Sergeant Schoolman.

"Now do you believe me?" Asked the Californian as two more VC ran by.

Schoolman brought his squad up on line.

"On my shot," commanded the sergeant as he and Burris moved forward as a fire team.

Schoolman saw movement and fired. The squad blasted the exposed enemy. Burris and Schoolman jolted forward. Pfc Richard Garner and Spec 4 Carl Klopfer laid down covering fire. Guerillas were firing from beneath a log. The green tracers streaked through the jungle shadows, chipping away at the massive anthill Burris was hiding behind. Garner appeared beside him. Together they concentrated fire at the Vietcong beneath the log, killing them with careful bursts. Garner then nudged Burris and signaled to move forward. For Burris, the movement seemed to take an eternity for just a few yards.

Four men moved forward, Garner, Klopfer, Burris, and Schoolman. The rest of the squad—Gardner, Peanuts, Ollie, Seasholtz were snail-pacing it off to the right. Garner and Klopfer were on their hands and knees, searching for cover. Intense fire caught them in the open. Klopfer raised up on his knees, saying, "There they are, down there!" He was shot immediately. He took a couple of rounds in the chest that spun him around. Before he hit the ground, he was nailed again in the neck.

Someone crawled forward to get Klopfer. Klopfer was dragged back. He had a sucking chest wound, shot through and through. Burris did not know Klopfer well but he had heard the stories about Klopfer taking a shower with his helmet on so mortars rounds would not hurt him, or the time on patrol when Klopfer accidentally fired the M79 grenade launcher he was carrying, striking the GI in line in front of him, but the grenade did not go off because it had not traveled far enough. Klopfer was a sad sack for sure, but Burris did not like to see anyone from the squad hit. A man down. Burris checked the position of the rest of the squad. They were stuck. They were not moving forward. The squad was pinned down.

Burris and Seasholtz grabbed the wounded man and attempted to "carry Klopfer to the center of the column for aid." Stumbling, struggling with the injured man's dead weight, a frustrated Seasholtz pushed Burris aside, lifted Klopfer, and carried him back toward the C.P.

Burris headed back to his position. Now there were other casualties. The Californian stopped to help a trooper hit in the elbow. The man's forearm and hand were swelling from the wound. Burris removed the G.I.'s wedding ring when the soldier said he thought he would lose both the ring and the finger. For Burris, it all seemed to be going sour.

When Steinberg's 4th Platoon moved up beside Kroah's 3rd Platoon, a gap appeared between the lead platoons and the 1st Platoon. Roger Harris listened as the firing to his front increased, though due to the jungle's thickness, it was impossible to see the two engaged platoons. Harris relates:

> "Some bullets whizzed through the air near Sergeant Sutterfield and me [Harris was the platoon sergeant's RTO] while we looked for the enemy off to our left flank. Bullets came from the opposite flank at my back and a tracer round briefly burned the ground near my feet."[51]

Reacting to the rising volume of fire, Sutterfield exclaimed, "Oh shit, we're surrounded!" He again searched out Captain Nolen. He attempted to explain to Nolen that the sniper fire "was actually to define our location, formation, and size."

1st Platoon was feeling the impact of the surging enemy. The enemy was attempting to drive through the company's center. One old hand on an M60 machine gun and his two green assistant gunners scrambled to take cover as the Vietcong concentrated a withering fire on them. Dust and leaves were kicking up from the heavy lead hitting the ground all about the American gunners. Tracers jumped toward the tree branches after ricocheting off the jungle floor.

Sergeant George Manning, an assistant gunner, lying on the ground and propped up on his elbows, was shouldering his M16 when the weapon spun from his hands after it was hit by small arms fire. In the next moment, Manning spilled onto his belly when a bullet disintegrated his left elbow. (Manning might have been the wounded soldier Burris would encounter in the coming minutes.)

The remaining two soldiers on the M60 worked the weapon with fierce determination, dropping several of their foes. The enemy's return fire was centered on silencing the automatic weapon. Pfc Leroy Tousant was ordered to take the gun after the old hand had lost the tips of two fingers from small arms fire. Tousant, a creole from Lake Charles, Louisiana, shouted back that he couldn't take the gun because he had been hit at the base of his neck.

With the machine gun down the guerillas hurried to fill the breach in the company's defenses. One VC darted past the wounded Americans and disappeared into the perimeter. Then three other attackers rose to make the assault. Though two made it past the three wounded Americans, the GI with the mangled hand was able to pop the last one as he attempted to run by. Another Vietcong began his dash only to be spotted by Sergeant Bradley, a new NCO to the platoon who hefted his rifle and loosed a round that sent the runner crashing to the ground. These aggressive infiltrators were attempting to establish the outlines of the American perimeter. By drawing fire that revealed the Americans' positions, the charging VC gave snipers a chance to pinpoint the Americans' position.[52]

Then the American artillery barrage began.

The barrage was the result of the 3rd Platoon's Lieutenant Kroah's quick reaction to the deteriorating situation. Conditioned by months of enemy hit-and-run tactics, Kroah had recognized that the galling gunfire drenching his unit was something different, something more, something more intense. Studying the peal of small arms fire, Kroah determined that his left flank, where Schoolman's squad was fighting, was taking the heaviest hits. He moved in that direction.

The lieutenant darted ahead of the men, Schoolman appearing beside him. The firing had metamorphosed into a wall of lead—after several minutes of combat 3rd Platoon was pinned down.

The words—or the gist of the words—from Major General DePuy to officers of the 1st Infantry Division when DePuy had taken command of the division began ringing in the lieutenant's mind, "You cannot be pinned down—You have too much artillery support to be pinned down. Any officer who reports that he is pinned down is going to get relieved right there." Kroah had to lay some heavy ordinance down on the Vietcong if he and his men were going to follow DePuy's orders.

DePuy's aggressive philosophy did not so much inspire Kroah with confidence in this situation as to condemn him to a single course of action. Contact was made, the firing was hot; time to blanket the enemy with some 105 mm HE (high explosive).

Kroah "...determined where most of the firing was coming from." Due to the vegetation in his immediate front, Kroah could see no more than ten yards, so deciding where the enemy's fire was coming from was an operation of calculated guessing. He listened to the gunfire and located the "hot spot;" he thought it was coming from a bunker. Kroah called the artillery forward observer, the practical-joking, always smiling

1st Lieutenant Francis (Frank) Fox—who was farther back in the column, traveling with the command group—on the PRC-25 radio and ordered a fire mission. Kroah told Schoolman to get back with his men. The sergeant refused.

"No, I'm not going to leave you."

The first round landed "a pretty good way out." Kroah instructed Fox to "drop fifty" yards. That next round went off to the right. Kroah was startled; it should have stepped in closer, straight in front of him. Using dead reckoning from what he heard, the lieutenant adjusted his coordinates and called the adjustments back to Fox. This third round careened off further out, beyond the first round. Concerned, Kroah adjusted again. This one came in close. Fine for killing VC. He ordered ten rounds for effect.

The 105 mm howitzer shells started hurtling in. One slammed into a tree to the left of Kroah's and Schoolman's position. The tree burst apart, sending deadly butcher knife-sized splinters ripping through the air. Another tree exploded in a bright blue flame that blossomed into a nightmarish roiling orange.

Then the screaming began. Two artillery rounds had hammered into the branches above the company's perimeter; the blasts chewed up Marty Kroah's men. Rifleman Wesley Carpenter, in Sergeant Corey's squad, was surrounded by blasted limbs "winging by," the sickening thump of a .51 caliber machine gun, and the howls of wounded men when a "big ass tree" took a hit from a shell and crashed down on him. "Part of a limb smashed my back, knocked me down, pinned me to the ground. I was knocked out. When I came to, I could not move or get up." Carpenter was now a witness to men in khakis maneuvering toward the torn-up 3rd platoon. Carpenter could only watch as Rifleman J.C. "Leslie" Short, of Jackson County, Michigan, stood up and charged the approaching enemy. A couple of other squad members followed. Carpenter could not believe his eyes and shouted for Short to stop, "Goddamn, Shorty, get down!" By then it was too late, Short (who was called Shorty because of his last name) was torn to pieces by enemy fire. From his vantage point further down the line, Richard Garner of Schoolman's squad saw the action as well, aghast that Short's uniform smoldered from the tracers that had dug into the G.I.

More shells pummeled the Americans' positions, the shrapnel slicing through the air above the company. Kroah shouted into the radio for the big guns to cease fire. Frank Fox had already radioed to the Fire Direction Center to adjust any more incoming rounds to high-angle fire. The change in orders came too late for many of Kroah's men. Dan Kirby, new to the company, watched a man die, the first man he had seen killed in combat, as the tree bursts tore up the unfortunate trooper.

..

Still, the fire mission had stymied the Vietcong assault on 1st Platoon, if inadvertently.

The company, already surprised and stunned by the enemy's resistance, convulsed as the barrage ceased. It was 1:45 PM. Each platoon had been taken under fire by snipers. Kroah's 3rd Platoon was reeling from multiple wounded. 4th Platoon, on Kroah's left flank, lay pinned down under heavy machine-gun fire; 1st Platoon had a machine gun crew knocked out; and 2nd Platoon, at the rear of the company, was reporting uniformed soldiers angling for cover just yards from their position. The company was reeling. Before the friendly fire had added to the number of wounded, Lieutenant Alderson and Captain Nolen in the command post had already realized that they had to get the company into a defensive perimeter to protect an evacuation site. At the rear of the columns,

Lieutenant Libs had, unbeknownst to Nolen, reached the same conclusion; the company had to squeeze back on itself and create a defensive perimeter. However, Libs' reasons for reaching this conclusion were different from his commander's conclusions. For the squads/platoons to remain strung out in the columns was to present the guerillas with an opportunity to surround each contingent and destroy it in detail. Libs jumped on his radio and bellowed, "Roll up the wagons and roll them up fucking now!"

---

*The company was using a formation known as "Platoon Line, Squads in Column." Rather than having each squad of a platoon follows one after the other, with each successive platoon doing the same in a single long column, the squads of a platoon were in multiple mutually supporting columns, with each successive platoon doing the same.

±Indeed, elements of the 5th Viet Cong Division, of which D800 was a component unit, had taken up positions to counter the Americans' presence the night of the contact. (Warren Wilkins, *Grab Their Belt to Fight Them*, (Annapolis, Naval Institute Press, 2011) 192.

**Sergeant Harold Hunter in 4th Platoon was thinking along the same lines as Lark. "Somebody was saying go down the path, I thought that was screwy, you never go down a path. You go across the path."

‡During the writing of this book, Pete Faberski voiced skepticism that Sergeant Sutterfield would have approached Nolan unbidden. In an e-mail, Faberski asserts, "Platoon Leaders and especially Platoon Sergeants did not go to the

command group location unless they were ordered to do so." Faberski did confirm in the same e-mail that Sutterfield was concerned about moving on the trails. Pete Faberski, e-mail, 8.24.04.

§In *Mud Soldiers* and my interviews with him, Marty Kroah identified his radio operator as Jasper Carpenter. There was no Jasper Carpenter in the unit. Marty merged his RTO's name and combined it with another soldier from his platoon, Wes Carpenter, for reasons that will become obvious as the story progresses. There was a Jasper Conway in the company at the time of the battle. He was from the South, and he was a radio man. Conway survived the fight on April 11 only to be killed toward the end of his tour in December.

Chapter Three: Roll up the Wagons

"In the minds of many Americans who fought in the Vietnam War…the Viet Cong…were supermen who could see in the dark, move silently and invisibly in all types of terrain, survive a week on a handful of rice, and willingly sacrifice their own lives if they could take a capitalist with them."

Col. Michael Lee Lanning Lt. Col. (RET); Dan Cragg. Inside the VC and the NVA: The Real Story of North Vietnam's Armed Forces

The terrain was ideal as a killing field. This area of Phuoc Tuy Province was "thick jungle," according to Harold D. Salem, a helicopter pilot who would have reason to know the nature of the vegetation shortly.[53] Tropical forest consisting of a phalanx of mammoth trees with interlocking branches that formed canopies above, while below was a scattering of second-growth trees and brush that were ubiquitous though not dense. The vines reached down from the limbs above, while below anthills rose from the jungle floor in freeform monuments to primordial survival. The ground was open enough beneath the trees that Dave Burris, walking point, had been able to pick his way around the above-ground roots and scrub bush without resorting to his machete. A soldier could see fifteen or twenty meters to his front and sides. Beyond those distances, the double canopy was enough to shut out all but thin shafts of sunlight, leaving most of the forest floor and underbrush in shadow. The scrub and the tall, wide anthills were just thick enough to obscure those who chose to hide there.

The soldiers were scrambling to scoop out defensive positions on land that sloped off to the west and south toward a streambed. 3rd and 4th platoons were facing west. Both platoons were lower on the slope than the 1st and 2nd platoons. And both 3rd and 4th platoons were just feet away from trenches—behind a tangle of vines and jumble of bamboo in their immediate front—where the VC had lined up two .51 caliber machine guns.[54] Beyond the machine guns and trenches was a Vietcong main force base camp loaded with troopers from the 274th Viet Cong Regiment. In the bushes fronting the slight knoll occupied by 1st and 2nd platoons were smaller caliber automatic weapons aimed at the Americans. Throughout the area—including what would become the company perimeter—snipers lurked in the trees.

The company had walked into an area made for an ambush.

Just under a quarter of all combat between Americans and the enemy in Vietnam were ambushes initiated by the enemy. More than twelve percent of engagements in the war involved American forces that stumbled across a VC position and attacked that position.[55] In C Company's case, their fight on April 11 was a search-and-destroy patrol that had stumbled upon the enemy, enticing the commander of the enemy regiment into an all-out assault to annihilate the American company.[56]

According to General John H. Hay, Jr., a search and destroy mission was "to locate...Vietcong main force units in and around their base areas and to attack them by fire and maneuver."[57] The reason for rooting out the enemy in their sanctuaries was to eliminate them in the countryside before they could attack the populated areas of South Vietnam. Theoretically, an enemy located in his base camp could be smashed using airstrikes, artillery barrage, and sometimes even naval fire. This method of dealing with the enemy would be codified in the "Big Red One Battle Principles," issued in 1967: first, "Infantry, armor, and Army aviation find the enemy." Next, "...artillery kill the enemy."[58] These principles meant that in General William DePuy's 1st Infantry Division, an actual assault by the infantry was considered a last resort. Finding the enemy, based on intelligence reports, was the infantry's job, not John Wayneing it into a base camp.[59*]

General DePuy used his own experience commanding a battalion in Europe during World War II to fashion the combat tactics used by his Big Red One in Vietnam. DePuy's evaluation of the American fighting man in World War II had not been favorable. DePuy's unit was part of the hard luck 90th Infantry Division, and the general felt that GIs had not shown enough aggressiveness on the battlefield. Given specific instructions, the American GI could accomplish much, but on their own, they lacked initiative and refused to take risks.

Couple the general's apprehension about the American fighting man's reluctance with a conviction that American artillery had been the "margin of superiority" in the war against the Germans, and the tactical use of search and destroy missions in Vietnam comes into focus. The foot soldiers were the hounds running their quarry to ground. Like hunting dogs, the riflemen were not to attempt to kill the prey but instead were to hold the hunted at bay until the artillery/airpower could strike and annihilate like a hunter come upon his howling dogs and their cornered prey.[60]

When Lieutenant Kroah had advised Captain Nolen to pursue the VC to determine their location—which the Lieutenant had done after the 3rd Platoon's point men had made contact—that advice was in line with search and destroy procedure. Charlie Company was in the jungle to find the enemy. When Sergeant Schoolman and his squad assaulted forward upon seeing the guerillas moving through the foliage, that maneuver was in keeping with running the enemy to ground (Schoolman recalls hooking into a squad on his right and expecting that squad to lay down a base of fire to cover Schoolman's assault. Platoon Sergeant Everett Eugene "Round Man" Langston had been with the platoon's rear elements and had moved the other squads into position quickly. But these units were taking so much fire as they moved to the line that it is doubtful that they provided suppressing fire for Schoolman's attack. They had their hands full fending off the enemy to their direct front.) When Kroah called for artillery, he was lifting a play from General DePuy's tactical playbook. So procedurally, in tick-off-the-list fashion, Charlie Company had done what was expected of a unit on a search and destroy mission.

Years later, General DePuy commented on the futility of search and destroy missions: "I was surprised a little bit...after I took over the division [at] the difficulty we had in trying to find the VC. They were more elusive. They *controlled* the battle better. They were the ones who decided whether there would be a fight."[61] (Italics added.) The general should not have been so surprised. In 1965, while he was General Westmoreland's Chief of Operations, the MACV staff reported that search and destroy missions were not working. Though the report was on the Army of the Republic of Vietnam (ARVN) failures, the conclusions reached in the report were that it was "the ability of the VC to break contact and 'disappear' from view" on their terms that was the deciding factor on whether contact was achieved during search and destroy missions.[62] As American units assumed the brunt of combat from the ARVN troops, General Westmoreland's evaluations based on U.S. operations confirmed that the guerillas were the ones deciding if combat was going to occur.[63]

So, though Company C had, up to that point, accomplished its mission, what the company was doing was only half the story; what the enemy was choosing to do was the other half.

According to Army Intelligence, the Vietcong in Phuoc Tuy Province had "...a well established intelligence system for...combat intelligence" within the province. An Intelligence report explained the ease with which the Vietcong could move through the entire region because, in essence, the province was their domain.[64] The guerillas used a series of trails that crisscrossed the province for communication and troop movements. The report confirmed the enemy's ability to move unseen by American eyes; "[d]espite constant surveillance [by U.S. forces], no significant VC movements were noted during daylight hours."[65]

The after-action report also confirmed in the specific instance of Phuoc Tuy Province what was acknowledged in general among the American military about contact with the enemy—the Vietcong would fight when and where they chose. And that the choice was predicated on their assessment of relative American weakness or tactical mistakes.[66] In "The Enemy," Donald R. Robinson wrote, "...he [the guerilla] is in his own country and his own environment; *he makes the rules.*"[67] (Emphasis added)

Evidence from the after-action report for Operation ABILENE and Viet Cong sources points to a scenario where the Vietcong chose when to make contact. American soldiers discovered several base camps during Operation ABILENE, but except for Charlie Company's find, these camps had been abandoned. Overall, contact with the enemy during the operation was sparse. The main targets of the American search, the 274th, and 275th Viet Cong Regiments were not even present in Phuoc Tuy at the time the operation began.[68] When contact did occur, it favored the guerillas.[69] Guerillas were taking potshots at the company that morning because Dang Ngoc Si, commander of the 274th had chosen to reveal his unit's whereabouts to the Americans.[70]

A review of pertinent information regarding Charlie Company's movements and the overall direction of Operation ABILENE verify that it was a conscious decision by the Vietcong commander to fight. Furthermore, it was a conscious decision on *how* the fight would unfold.[71]

The operation had been ongoing since March 30, yet the after-action report pointed out that the enemy had managed to avoid significant contact.[72] Considering the VC intelligence network's soundness in the area, the enemy tracked American movements from the first day of the operation. Such a network allowed the enemy to use standard guerilla tactics, simply melting away into the jungle when a large U.S. force drew near. However, the Army's intelligence assessment warned that the Vietcong would strike quickly if the enemy judged that they had "achieved tactical surprise as well as numerical superiority."[73] Therefore, though the guerillas were undoubtedly avoiding contact that was not to their advantage, they were also scouting U.S. units for an opportunity to attack.

Recall that on April 10, one of the three enemy scouts spotted and assaulted by Charlie Company had escaped. The company XO, Lieutenant Ken Alderson, had been primarily concerned that the escaped scout would relay the company's whereabouts to a larger Vietcong unit. That is what happened, as the Vietcong sent out more scouts to track the Americans while the rest of the regiment took up positions to fight.[74] When General DePuy had swooped into the area in his helicopter, he too had warned that an enemy attack was imminent. It was as simple as the enemy knowing the company's position. It turned out there was no attack that night, but the enemy had an eye on Company C and was waiting for the right moment to strike.

Even if the escaped scout had not reported the discovery of the Americans and even if the company's move from one edge of the field to another had fooled any other scouts, Charlie Company's march through the jungle the following morning provided several opportunities for early warning. Consider the unit's turn westward at 11 AM.[75] If Dang Ngoc Si was attempting to wait out the operation, hoping that the Americans would bypass the battalion base camp by heading to the east of it, the turn westward alerted the VC officers that the Americans were moving directly toward the base. Evacuation of the base could have commenced at that time. However, to stretch credulity, perhaps the enemy did not have eyes on Charlie Company at the time of the westward turn; the commander of

D800 would have soon been notified of the GIs' approach because of what happened next.

Just minutes after the turn westward at 11 AM, the company discovered a well-traveled jungle trail.[76] This event occurred at 11:15. At that time, Captain Nolen sent out patrols to scout the area. Since the trail ran east-west and thus directly into D800's base camp, it can be assumed that the Vietcong watched it.[±] At that time, even if no one at the base camp had been aware of the Americans' movement until that moment, the guerilla leader had plenty of time to evacuate the base camp if that was the plan. The ABILENE after-action report states that 1st Infantry Division forces had uncovered several abandoned base camps during the operation. It was commonly accepted among the Americans that the Vietcong could disappear from base areas at a moment's notice.[77] If the 274th Regiment's leader had wanted to slip away from the Americans, he could have completed the maneuver at that time.

Once the company patrols came back reporting no enemy, Nolen's men moved out again. They moved west until approximately noon, then stopped for lunch. By 12:15, Burris and another soldier had spotted trail watchers, and 3rd Platoon's Lieutenant Kroah had informed Captain Nolen that his platoon had made contact. The company sat there for several minutes more as Nolen instructed Kroah to patrol forward and make contact again. This command again provided the Vietcong opportunity to escape through the base camp's back door had the guerilla leader chosen to do so. Instead, Dang Ngoc Si chose to fight at the base camp entrance because he had been watching the Americans, knew their strength, and knew that support from other American units was too far off to allow for immediate assistance.[**] Knowing those things allowed the VC commander the latitude to order his men to stop Kroah's men at the front of the Company's position and surround the entire unit.

It was not a classic Vietcong ambush, well-planned and rehearsed, but rather an impromptu action by a resourceful and quick-thinking commander following the Vietcong's basic directives to seek out and take advantage of American missteps. Spontaneous or planned meant the same thing in practical terms for the company. They had walked into deadly Vietcong fields of fire. The Americans were virtually surrounded and out of reach of practical support.

Phil Hall certainly felt isolated. Even before the rain of friendly artillery fire had come crashing into the company's position, the Pfc, out beyond 2nd Platoon's left flank, was trapped under the inaccurate but still dangerous gunfire of two infiltrators. Lieutenant Libs called out for Hall to get into the perimeter. Hall bounded up to attempt a sprint under the enemy's guns. "A [VC] behind a termite mound stood up and started advancing toward me;" Hall recalled. The guerilla was between Hall and the relative safety of the perimeter. Hall leveled his shotgun and blasted the man. Then the Pfc ran.

Fire from an AK47 drove Hall diving for cover behind an anthill. As he tumbled behind the scant shelter, a soldier named Rick Owens, who had already found refuge behind the anthill, asked Hall if he was hit. "'Fuck no,' I said and I rolled and kept going" toward the perimeter with the AK47 pounding bullets at Hall the entire way. Owens was busy with his special piece of hell as moments before Hall appeared another soldier, pinned down by sniper fire, bellowed, "can you see him?" Owens responded that he could and took careful aim at a point high up in a tree and jabbed a round into the air. The sniper fell from the upper branches but hung suspended from a rope attached to the tree.

Meanwhile, Hall made it to the perimeter, but his friend Specialist 4 John Noyce had been caught outside the lines as the unit recoiled. "I was out there behind a tree by myself." Luckily for Noyce, Lieutenant Libs was missing a machine gun, and Noyce was carrying one.

"'Get your ass in here, Noyce!' Libs commanded. 'We need the 60.'"[78]

Because of Libs' order and Hall's encouragement – Hall had yelled to Noyce that if he [Hall] could make it, so could Noyce – the machine gunner hoisted the M60 and bolted toward the perimeter. Once in the perimeter, Noyce positioned the machine gun on the knoll.

Labeling the area that the company occupied a "perimeter" is a matter of literary convenience rather than accuracy. There was no neat line with interlocking fields of fire. Combat's thunderclap shocked the platoons. As 1st and 2nd platoons pushed into the available cover, communications between platoons—between squads and even between men—shattered.

In 1st Platoon's area (to the west or "in front" of the 2nd Platoon), new trooper Pfc Kenneth Mize was firing his .45 caliber pistol at any movement in the brush. Snipers' bullets and automatic fire poured toward him in a torrent. Mize felt terribly alone, hunkered down in a position where he could not see another American soldier. Finally, Mize caught a glimpse of Sergeant George Manning gripping his bloody elbow as he stumbled away from the incoming blaze of fire. Yet Manning was soon gone, and Mize was alone again. Over the din of gunfire, Mize heard Staff Sergeant John L. Bradley shout, "I hit one between the eyes," but the Arkansan could not see the non-com. Equipped with an M79 grenade launcher,‡ which was useless in the patch of jungle where Mize was seeking cover, the soldier waited for the non-coms to straighten things out while he continued to shoot at any movement to his front.

Not far from Mize, Specialist 4 Doug Blankenheim of 1st Platoon was busy trying to stay alive as he too experienced the individual nature of the fight:

"People were inside the perimeter, outside the perimeter and we were trying to get a force to sustain ourselves. I remember everyone was hitting the ground, taking up positions, and laying down a field of fire. I was selectively firing. I was trying to find targets. [I hit] one...for sure. He was about fifteen feet from me...I shot him right through the head. He was crawling toward me and came over a log, and I shot him. I saw one running. I don't know if I hit him or not."

As Blankenheim methodically triggered his M16, a sergeant positioned behind him went berserk. The severity of the incoming fire, coupled with the misplaced U.S. artillery, had rattled the NCO. Blankenheim remembers: "This sergeant started screaming that we were all going to die because we were really getting hit hard. Artillery and mortars were coming down. He was behind me. I went back to try and get him squared away..." The sergeant was standing, screaming at the top of his lungs. Blankenheim risked the incoming fire by racing back and tackling the non-com. Blankenheim, an amiable soldier with a solid reputation in the company, wrestled the man down. The Spec 4 pinned and slapped the sergeant to calm the man. The sergeant continued to thrash about uncontrollably until shrapnel from the errant artillery rounds tore into Blankenheim's thigh and buttocks, the jolt causing the ranting NCO to go limp under Blankenheim.

Blankenheim was slammed by a searing pain lancing through his backside. Someone, possibly the sergeant, called for a medic. Blankenheim had the wherewithal to know he was not dying, but the wounded GI still had a reason for concern. Beyond the pain was the need to know that "the boys," his testicles, were still intact. Once the medic had reassured him that he could father children, Blankenheim picked up a discarded M16 (The same artillery burst that had wounded him had destroyed his weapon) and, despite his wounds, took up a fighting position once again.

Blankenheim was not the only 1st Platoon soldier hit by the short artillery rounds. Pfc Bobby Holton, one of the youngsters Platoon Sergeant Hugh Sutterfield sought to protect by assigning them relatively safer jobs within the platoon,[§] was Lieutenant Smith DeVoe's RTO. When the artillery began slamming into the trees, there were no secure areas within the platoon; a piece of shrapnel fell across Holton's legs. Though the shrapnel did not penetrate the legs, it burned them severely. Simultaneously, another hunk of metal sliced across Holton's chest, scraping a bloody path across the skin.

The short rounds were creating chaos in 1st Platoon. Platoon Sergeant Hugh Sutterfield and weapons squad sergeant Pete Faberski, who as a child had experienced the Soviet destruction of Berlin, were blown against some bamboo. "It shook us up. You could see dirt and branches raining down on us. Men in the platoon were screaming, 'Stop this shit, make it stop.' The artillery fire really did us in," Faberski remembers. "All of a sudden we had a bunch of wounded," and Faberski and Sutterfield—both of whom were miraculously unhurt from the concussion that had slammed them into the bamboo—knew that the jungle did not afford any place to land helicopters to get those wounded out.

Instantly, the 1st Platoon NCOs were trying to make sense of the confusion. Sergeant John Bradley—who had already proclaimed that he had bagged one VC by shooting him between the eyes—began to move among the men, encouraging them, pointing out targets, providing proof to the GIs that they were not alone in those fiery moments when death seemed to be descending on them.[79]

Platoon Sergeant Sutterfield was also hustling to establish contact with his men. Pfc Mize—who was still potting away at the enemy with his .45—watched as Sutterfield was quickly in motion, calling out for the men to spread out and directing others to better cover. The sergeant plugged holes in the lines by moving the men about, but despite Sutterfield's actions, this perimeter was more a collection of individual fighting positions than a battle line.

Sergeant Faberski got word that one of his machine guns had been knocked out.[§§]

"You better get over there, Hoss," Sutterfield ordered Faberski, whom Sutterfield invariably called 'Hoss,' "See what's going on. We need that gun."

Ordered to find the machine gun amid the carnage of battle, Faberski low-walked/crawled in the direction where the machine gun had last been located. Faberski came across the fire team leader for 1st Squad, Sergeant James Robinson of Hinsdale, Illinois. Both NCOs flattened on the ground. Robinson was animated and excited, his eyes boring into Faberski. "I dropped one out there," Robinson told Faberski. Robinson wanted to crawl out to where he believed the body lay, to confirm the kill. The fire was too intense for such a venture. Faberski did not have to ask Robinson about the situation with the M60; Robinson yelled that the crew had been knocked out. Then the former Marine, a man who had vowed to earn a Medal of Honor, told Faberski not to worry about the machine gun. Robinson already had another crew working it. Faberski turned back to find Sutterfield and Lieutenant DeVoe.

The M60 that was the cause of Faberski's mission was now manned by Pfcs Ron Haley, Alvin Brown, and Robert "Tator" Rohl. Rohl had been with the company a week and a day.

Particular Bravery: The Battle of Xa Cam My And The Death of a Grunt Company

Brown recalls that the landscape was already alien from the typical Vietnam battlefield: "The area was like a scene from WWI with shell holes, bomb craters, torn and broken trees everywhere." Brown remembers the oppressive jungle darkness that hid everything from view except the green tracers of the enemy fire that seemed to zero in on him.

Haley also felt the heat from the incoming rounds and instructed Brown to dig a foxhole while Rohl and he [Haley] provided covering fire. A few moments later, Rohl tapped Haley on the shoulder and pointed to a madly digging Brown. Haley smiled and called out, "Hey, Alvin, if you're not going to use your shovel, can I use it?" Brown had been frantically hacking at the ground with his helmet instead of using his entrenching tool. "Poor Alvin got a sheepish look on his face, put his steel pot on, grabbed his entrenching tool, and continued digging. Considering the situation at the time, the three of us laughing like idiots must have seemed a little out of place to anybody watching."[80]

The laughter was short-lived. The fire was too intense in that relatively open area, so Haley went leaping forward over a log, and the overweight Brown could only manage to "sort of roll over it [the log]." Yet Brown stayed with Haley as the Californian took up a position behind another log. Haley poured out the fire until he had used up his last belt of ammunition. Then he pulled open the M60's feed tray, and with unrepeatable and unpracticed dexterity, Brown heaved an ammo belt at the weapon and was amazed that the belt landed perfectly into the feed tray. Haley slammed the tray shut and recommenced firing.

Haley had positioned the machine gun more for cover than for a clear field of fire. Although the log the Americans were behind was on the slight slope on the company's left flank (so Haley had the "high ground"), he never saw the enemy. He noticed a massive limb suspended over the log just as a short round smashed into it, causing the limb to crash down virtually on top of the three Americans. Haley never wore a helmet, preferring the boonie hat typical of camp wear and that sartorial choice was going to cost him there in the jungle. The blast that ripped down the limb above him also knocked Haley several feet, and though he crawled back to the M60 and continued firing, he was disoriented and dizzy for most of the remainder of the battle.

Medic Bob Fisher was busy in the 2nd Platoon's area crawling between the mounting numbers of wounded. Fisher was returning from the back of the columns, where he had treated a GI shot in the back when he happened upon a guy who matter-of-factly said, "Hey, doc, come here a minute." The soldier was lying down in a fighting position, but Fisher could see that the man had been shot in the arm. Fisher crawled over and saw that the arm was busted up and limp. Fisher patched the arm as best he could and gave the trooper a shot of morphine.

"We'll get you out soon," Fisher reassured the wounded man.

One 2nd Platoon soldier that Fisher did not treat was Sergeant Passmore, the same non-com that had straightened out the medic regarding why the company had cut loose on the VC scouts on Easter. Passmore had made his way to the CP area for evacuation after being hit in the leg by shrapnel. The company had lost one of its most combat-savvy leaders.

Further down that slope in 4th Platoon's area, there was serious trouble. The ground ran down toward the southwest, which put the 4th Platoon lower than any other American unit. The enemy's entrenched .51 caliber machine gun was keeping the unit's collective heads down. 4th Platoon was no longer advancing; they were holding on.

With the initial blast from the .51 caliber, Sergeants Harold Hunter and Bozy Gerald had hurled themselves to the ground. In the months Hunter had been in Vietnam, he and Gerald had bonded in an almost father-son relationship, with the much older Gerald referring to Hunter as "Young Buck Sergeant" and Hunter looking to Gerald for advice and approval. Now, as the big rounds from the .51 tore into the ground around him, Hunter felt something sharp scratch across one of his arms. He glanced at his arm, expecting to see a shrapnel or bullet wound; instead, he saw the end of a branch brushing against his sleeve. The branch was long, with a splintered end as if it had been blasted off a tree by a machine gun. At the other end of the limb was a smiling Staff Sergeant Gerald.

Hunter could not quite manage a grin of his own, but he did raise the fingers on his right hand an inch, just enough to acknowledge Gerald's prodding. Laying there with the side of his face pressed into the dirt, the younger sergeant recalled how Gerald, his Vietnam mentor, had told him some months earlier, "if we ever get in trouble, but can't talk to each other, find a stick or some pebbles and let the other guy know you're alive." Gerald was adamant that the two stick together and always let the other know they were not alone. As Hunter listened to the sickening thud of the .51 caliber slugs sinking into soft tissue and then the "momentary moans or gasping" of the dying all around him, he was grateful that Gerald was beside him.

..

3rd Platoon was still under the gun on 4th Platoon's right. Snipers were keeping the men ducking. Pfc John (Ollie) Lang of Sergeant Schoolman's squad had sought cover behind a huge log. Schoolman and Randall "Peanuts" Prinz was there. Lang watched as Seasholtz and Burris hustled the wounded Spec 4 Klopfer toward the rear of the column. The log seemed to be taking fire from three sides. Lang glanced toward his right to see a soldier hefting his M16 over the top of the log and firing blindly, never lifting his head over the top of the log. Even that precaution did not protect the GI—a bullet shattered his hand. The wounded soldier followed Burris and Seasholtz back toward the remains of the company.[81]

After what seemed an eternity, the hostile fire drifted. It was after 2:00 PM. In 3rd and 4th Platoon's areas, any exposure could get a trooper shot, but the intensity of the fire had slackened. Both Lieutenant Kroah and Platoon sergeant Eugene "Round Man" Langston headed back toward the company command post to check on their wounded.

Sergeant Langston happened upon the wounded Doug Blankenheim, still dutifully manning a defensive position despite the wounds to his rear. "You hit?" asked Langston.

"I got hit," responded Blankenheim. "I'm sure I'm OK. I can walk."

"You're getting out of here. You got any ammo?" Langston asked. The sergeant relieved the wounded GI of his gear and then directed him toward the command post.

Near a mammoth fallen tree in 2nd Platoon's area, Nolen and his XO, Ken Alderson, had established the command post and were also busy organizing the clearing of some kind of landing zone. Men used their machetes to hack at bamboo and saplings. The healthy GIs slashed away at the brush; the wounded filtered back to the area on their own, or the seriously injured, like Spec 4 Carl Klopfer, were carried by their fellow GIs. The work was overwhelming; the jungle was too thick for a feasible landing zone. Removing saplings and other brush cleared the jungle floor but did nothing to penetrate the canopy above. Nolen received radio directions to cut a hole through the canopy. Since there was no place to land a helicopter, jungle penetrators would be used from hoist-equipped helicopters to get litters down to the wounded.

Lieutenants Smith DeVoe of 1st Platoon and George Steinberg of 4th Platoon made it to the CP area. Steinberg showed off the wound on his arm, a gash five or six inches long that was not particularly bothersome. Steinberg made a point of telling the company's tactical communications chief, Sergeant Charles Weyant, that he [Steinberg] "just got my Purple Heart!" and then showed Weyant the wound. Once the wound was dressed, Steinberg headed back to his platoon.

Smith DeVoe's assessment of the situation as the firing slackened was that it had been a sharp engagement, but the fighting was over. "We took some heavy hits [but] we shot the Hell out of them [the guerillas], we put in a lot of artillery around here," and combat was over. Things had calmed down.

Medic Bob Fisher was as sure that "it" was over. The scene at the CP was confused but not chaotic. Lieutenant Libs and others were expecting Fisher to decide who should be evacuated first. Fisher felt making that kind of decision was a burden, but there were other medics, like Dave Marchetti, to share that burden. Still, the number of wounded was daunting. They littered the area. Their cries were tortured, while the grotesque nature of the two dead GIs' wounds repulsed the living.

Company XO Ken Alderson suggested that Captain Nolen order an ammunition resupply since the company had burned through their ammunition in the heat of the fight – better to get resupplied than be caught with too little ammunition. The Army helicopter dutifully appeared soon after the request but attempted to beg off dropping the ammunition because it could not identify the company's location.

Lieutenant Kroah, angry and anguished, grabbed a handset and, through clenched teeth, told the helicopter pilot that if the drop didn't happen, he (Kroah) would shoot down the chopper. Alderson listened as the helicopter came buzzing in just over the tree tops kicking crates out of the cabin. The XO grimaced as a box of ammunition came crashing down through the trees to land with a sickening thud onto a GI corpse.

Spec 4 Howard Blevins, a soft-spoken draftee and an RTO in Sergeant Charles Weyant's communications unit, had several friends in the 3rd Platoon and took the ammunition resupply as an opportunity to check up on them. The specialist grabbed several cans of M60 machine gun ammunition, telling Sergeant Weyant that he was heading to the 3rd Platoon. Blevins never returned to the communications unit.

By 3:00 PM, things had stabilized all around the perimeter. The company was now more or less in an elliptical perimeter, with the long axis running east to west and the short axis running north to south. The 3rd and 4th platoons nailed down the western end of the perimeter, with the 3rd on the right flank and Steinberg's 4th on the left flank while the 1st Platoon was wedged up against Steinberg's platoon on the east and Libs' 2nd Platoon protected Kroah's platoon's rear. Above the jungle, Major Bibb Underwood, the Battalion XO, hovering in a copter from the 2nd Brigade, relayed information from headquarters to Charlie Company and vice versa. Underwood let Nolen know that the Air Force was on its way. The company had managed to chop out a hole in the jungle large enough for an Air Force Kaman HH-43F (Huskie) to lower itself to within a hundred feet of the ground. From there, the helicopter crew could drop a Stokes basket (a metal-framed stretcher with raised sides) through the canopy to the small clearing below. That way the wounded could be evacuated with the chopper never risking a landing.[82]

The command post (CP) had been established near the junction of the 3rd and 4th platoons with the wounded congregated there as well. 2nd Platoon's Bob Fisher watched as a "large silver bird" came hovering over the jungle. A cable with a litter attached descended from the silver helicopter (David E. Milsten, a pararescue man who was operating in one of the two "Huskie" copters on the mission, described the Huskie as "an upside down egg beater," with "the rotor blades actually intermeshed with each other—it looked like a disaster waiting to happen.")[83] Fisher and one or two of the ambulatory wounded struggled to get one of the more severely injured men into the Stokes litter. The medic had no training on how to control the swinging basket, and the wounded soldier had a shaky ride up, almost falling out of the litter as he ascended to the belly of the Husky. The Husky flew up and out of the hole and was immediately replaced by a second copter, also a Husky. Another wounded soldier was loaded into the litter, but as with the first casualty, there were complications with getting this soldier securely into the stretcher. Captain Harold D. Salem, the pilot of the second Husky observed the soldiers wrestling with the basket; "Once they figured out how to rig the sling assembly, they placed a wounded soldier, stretcher and all in the Stokes litter."[84]

Salem described the scene below and its consequences:

> "They [the soldiers] reattached the sling and gave us the thumbs up for hoisting. The stretcher had been made from a poncho and two long tree limbs.
> They had done the...best they could under existing conditions; however, it really complicated the pickup because the [makeshift] stretcher poles extending out of the Stokes litter on both ends caused the...litter to continually get hung up in the [tree branches defining the tight space of the hole.]"[85]

The impromptu nature of the long stretcher poles hampered getting the wounded man into the helicopter cabin. The crew "had to swing the stokes litter out far enough and away from the chopper before they could bring the patient in feet first."[86] Finally, the crew managed to get the litter partially into the cabin but it then took up so much space that the pararescue team could not pick up another wounded trooper.[87] Pedro 97 then dropped back in the hole and retrieved a second wounded soldier. The two helicopters then flew to a field hospital a few miles away to deliver the three wounded men. This initial segment of the rescue mission had taken an excruciating forty-five minutes to complete.[88]

As the slicks disappeared with the wounded, on the ground Fisher was treating the wounded and pulling them into the small clearing so that when the Air Force copters returned he could have the men ready to go. When one of the aircraft finally did materialize in the hole through the jungle canopy Fisher explained what happened next:

> "The basket had...been lowered again. This time though, one of the paramedics was with it. As I came in closer, I saw a young airman, uniform [clean] and neatly worn, showing another medic how to properly strap in the wounded. He [the pararescue airman] was carrying a .38 in a holster and appeared out of place in the jungle. I soon found that he fit right in...'Nice weapon,' I said to him as he was instructing us on lift procedure, 'Did you buy it yourself?' 'Yeah,' he said,
>
> 'I bought it just for the occasion. Never used it though.'"[89]

The airman in the clean uniform was Airman First Class (A1C) William Pitsenbarger, known as "Bill" or "Pits" to his friends. That day the native of Piqua, Ohio, was assigned to the 2nd alert crew for the Aerospace Rescue and Recovery Squadron, Detachment 6 (Det 6), at Bien Hoa. Acting as a member of the 2nd alert crew meant Pits was free from one of the normal duties of a pararescue airman. The unit's usual mission was to rescue downed pilots and when not committed to that dangerous responsibility, to also act as firemen for combat-battered planes landing at the air base. The 1st alert crew for Det 6 was handling the crash support work that day so Pits was enjoying something of an easy day when the Army's call for help came in at approximately 3 PM. Occasionally, the Air Force's highly trained pararescue teams were called in to retrieve Army wounded, but typically, that was for "one or two casualties" since the Husky helicopter was a relatively small aircraft.[90] For such off-base rescue missions, the copters operated in pairs, which meant Pits' 2nd alert crew in Pedro 73 joined Pedro 97 (Pedro was the call sign for these choppers), as the rescue mission got underway.[91] Later, Airman Second Class (A2C) Roy A. "Frenchy" Boudreaux, Pits' roommate, recalled the 21 year-old taking a moment as he scrambled toward Pedro 73 to say "I have a bad feeling about this mission."[92] If Pits was apprehensive about the mission that was uncharacteristic of him. According to rescue pilot Captain Dale Potter, who knew Pitsenbarger, the airman "was always willing to get into the thick of the action where he could be the most help."[93] He had already logged 250 such missions during his time in-country.

On the ground, Fisher got the impression that the airman was dropped down to organize the evacuation because the first wounded man had nearly fallen from the Stokes litter. The Army medic was exactly right. The crew of Pedro 73 had debated the sad results of the first pickup. It was Pits who came up with a solution. The airman volunteered to run the rescue from the ground.[94]

Fisher and the other medics certainly welcomed Pitsenbarger's calm demeanor and clear instructions. The airman organized things and began moving the wounded up into the helicopters faster than the GIs could have done alone. However, the Huskies were not built to carry large loads, one of two wounded at the most. This meant the helicopters had to hoist up their human cargoes individually or in pairs and shuttle them to an airstrip approximately eight miles from the action, then return for more wounded.[95] The Air Force choppers made three trips this way, with one or two wounded per helicopter per trip. This laborious process meant that the evacuation was taking a long time. Fisher worried that the shooting might start up again before all the wounded had made it out of the jungle.

That Pitsenbarger was even on the ground during the evacuation was astonishing to the men of Charlie Company. Lieutenant Libs thought the airman was insane to descend onto the battleground. "We knew we were in the fight of our lives and my knees were shaking, and I just couldn't understand why anybody would put himself in this grave danger if he didn't have to." Phil Hall watched in awe as Pitsenbarger descended. It was the "...most unselfish and courageous act I ever witnessed."[96]

Beyond the perimeter, the VC's regimental commander was taking note of the drawn-out evacuation process. He looked at his watch more than once as the Air Force helicopters flew in and out. He registered that the American flankers had been driven in. He awaited word from his various trail watchers—his eyes on the other American companies hunting him—word of movement in his direction. Had the other American units reacted to Charlie Company's plight? He eyed the lengthening shadows as well, judging the coming of dusk.

With things seemingly under control at the evacuation area, Sergeant Langston began carefully picking his way back toward the 3rd Platoon at the front of the perimeter. Along the way, Langston happened upon 1st Platoon's Sergeants Hugh Sutterfield and Pete Faberski. In his inimitable style, the Round Man produced a can of Falstaff beer. The three friends were prone on the ground—there were still errant rounds occasionally zinging the air—sharing the beer and discussing the situation. Langston told the other two about the men he had lost and cursed the short rounds. Sutterfield and Faberski reciprocated. Two or three minutes between friends. "While we were drinking it [the beer]," Faberski recalls that a staccato burst of fire suddenly filled the air. "Langston was joking, 'I'm going to get the Hell out of here, your area is getting a little too hot for me.' And with those words, he departed." He grinned his quirky little grin and was gone. Faberski and Sutterfield would not see Langston alive again.

The shooting that had hastened Langston's departure was general along the perimeter. The Vietcong commander had received reports from his scouts, no American movement in the direction of the base camp. The other Army units were preparing their night perimeters. The enemy leader checked that his soldiers were in position, firmly ringing in the Americans. The machine guns were in place, the mortars were ready, and the snipers were situated. Dusk was approaching. He ordered the attack.‡‡

At the CP, the guerillas opened up. 1st Platoon's Lieutenant Smith DeVoe remembers, "The world erupted." The guerillas aimed at one of the Huskies. The order was given for A1C Pitsenbarger to take the next ride on the hoist up to the helicopter. He had done his duty. "'Pits' chose to stay with the wounded, giving up his ride to safety."[97] Pedro 73 was on its sixth run to the battle site when machine-gun fire cut a bundle of wiring in the helicopter, causing the throttle to stick on the open position. The descending litter "went crashing through the trees, threatening to tangle the line and pivot the helicopter into the ground." The pilot, Harold D. Salem, "sheared the cable, and the damaged chopper limped back to its base."[98]

"It was a surprise to me—when so many men on the ground would have given anything to be somewhere else—that this guy [Pitsenbarger] chose to stay with the Company," Fisher marveled. Fisher went up to the airman and inquired when Pitsenbarger was going to go up. The airman simply said, "Later."

If the guerilla leader's unfolding plan worked, there would be no later. Just as the ground was ideal for killing, the hour and the opportunity had converged to make dusk of April 11, 1966, the perfect killing time.

Nolen ordered the platoons to "tighten up" their lines into a perimeter while the captain also radioed Kroah.[99]

"Look, we're getting out of here," Nolen told Kroah, referring to the company's pulling back into a more defensive position. "Get your men together and get ready to go."

Kroah responded, "Hey, there's no way, I've got more wounded men than men capable of carrying 'em out."

"You better figure out something 'cause we're moving out."

Nolen's dismissive statement pissed off Kroah. The lieutenant believed his platoon was being abandoned. George Wilson, writing about the battle in his book *Mud Soldiers*, concurred. "Nolen ordered his platoons to pull back from the most intense fire…He hoped to avoid encirclement of the whole company even if he had to lose the point platoon…that was…in danger of being overrun."[100]

Kroah was soon called to the radio again. Nolen again. Kroah listened as the nervous captain said, "We're not going anywhere."

The Vietcong positioned to the 3rd Platoon's front were not yet spent. Charlie Company's soldiers had yet to feel the full impact of an enemy smelling blood, tasting death. The Americans could not know that their stand in a nasty little patch of jungle east of Saigon was about to feel the sting of the VC way of war.

---

*John Wayneing it: slang for acting macho or like a hero. Linda Reinberg, *In the Field: The Language of the Vietnam War*. (New York: Facts On File, Inc., 1991.), 117.

±According to a MACV document from 1968, *Counterinsurgency Lessons Learned, No.68: Vietcong Base Camps and Supply Caches,* base camps were guarded by well-trained troops.

** In R. P. Harrison's unpublished article, *"Mapping Jungle Trails,"* operational instructions from higher up were for companies to patrol with 600 meters between units. However, 2nd Brigade procedure in past operations had been a standard 400 meters between companies. Author George Wilson stated that Bravo Company, 2/16 was 1000 meters away from Charlie Company when the fight began. Certainly, the company was too isolated for robust support.

‡The M79 grenade launcher uses 40x46 mm grenades that "have fuses that activate at or past 30 m, as a safety precaution; as such, a grenadier armed with an M79 and fighting closer targets will either have to use a buckshot or canister round, directly hit an enemy soldier with a grenade, or switch to a different weapon. When fired, the M79 has a distinct muzzle report similar in sound to a cork being pulled out of a bottle; for

this reason, it became widely-known" as a "'Blooper' and 'Thumper'". "M79," *Military-Today.com*, https://military-today.com/firearms/m79.htm, accessed 10. 20. 2022.

§Sutterfield had assigned the youngest member of Charlie Company, Roger Harris, as his own RTO. Radiomen traveled close to their assigned charge, and in many cases, this meant the middle of the column. The downside to being a radio operator was that the long antennae alerted the enemy to your presence, and they were particularly interested in knocking the radio out to inhibit communications.

§§Faberski was in charge of both of 1st Platoon's M60 machine guns.

‡‡The actions of the VC commander described here are in keeping with known Vietcong tactics. As a soldier from Company B, 2nd Battalion, 18th Infantry Regiment, PFC Gilford Bender, noted at the time, "That VC commander planned it so he could whack Charlie Company real good right before sunset." – "Mapping Jungle Trails," R. P. Harrison.

Chapter Four:
The Descent

"I knew I was going to die."

John (Combat Ollie) Lang

"I just gave up. I prayed to God to take me. Take me now."

Marty Kroah

"Is this the way you die?"

Richard Garner

"I ain't going to make it back."

F. David Peters

"We're all dead."

Smith DeVoe

The dizzying drop into a nightmare was disorienting; the volume of lead and death that swallowed the company; it was, as well, the sheer rapidity and steep pitch of the descent that compounded the confusion.

In the 3rd Platoon's area, Sergeant Schoolman's squad, Burris, Lang, and the others, continued to huddle behind the big log that lay halfway down the slope between the enemy trenches and the remainder of the company. Jammed against the log, Burris noticed a soldier resting his M16 on top of the deadfall firing the rifle blindly, never raising his head. Burris thought that was an excellent way of returning fire without getting his head blown off, so he hefted his M16 over the top of the log and let loose with a sweeping burst. Schoolman went "ape-shit."

"Goddamn it, don't fire unless you see a target!"

Obeying the sergeant's order, Burris and John (Ollie) Lang began a deadly game of jungle shooting gallery. The GIs acted both as shooters, popping up over the log to fire, and then becoming the targets, as fire came careening in at them as they poked their heads over that log. Because of the fusillade of incoming fire, it was a game the two GIs realized they were bound to lose. Fortunately, the word came down to cease fire because the 4th Platoon was sweeping in front of the 3rd Platoon's lines to retrieve Pfc Marion Acton's body (Acton was the first Charlie Company soldier killed during the 4th Platoon's initial contact with the enemy).

4th Platoon's wounded Lieutenant George Steinberg (he had received a grazing wound on his arm during the first burst of enemy fire) and his RTO braved a rising volume of small arms fire to attempt to recover Acton's body. They alternated sprinting and crawling out of the perimeter into no man's land. As the two Americans reached the body, it became evident to Steinberg that he needed more manpower to get the body and himself out of a steadily worsening situation. While seeking cover where there was essentially no cover, he radioed back to Lieutenant Kroah for help.

"I knew where he was," Kroah explained, "because I could hear the firing [to his front] "I turned to three or four of my men and said [pointing at individuals] you, you and you, come on, follow me. I took off. I got to George and looked back and there was nobody there!" No member of his platoon had followed Kroah.

"That was a funny feeling. I grabbed the dead guy's weapon, George and the other soldier straddled the guy's [the body's] arms and started dragging him and I used his weapon and my weapon and simply just recon-by-fire, firing single shots out of each weapon, back and forth."

With the butts of the M16s jammed against his hips as he fired, Kroah raked the jungle as he backed up as quickly as he could. With Kroah covering the retreat, Steinberg was able to get Acton's body back to the perimeter.

Steinberg found a spot at the end of the log next to Burris. Steinberg talked excitedly to Burris, but the enlisted man couldn't make out the officer's words. It was almost as if Steinberg was in shock, talking incoherently. As for Burris, he stared at Steinberg's blood-soaked fatigues, and again the feeling that things were bad, really bad, overwhelmed the Californian. The Pfc felt as if he was merely an observer to the mess, listening but not hearing the babbling lieutenant, seeing but not registering that beyond the end of the log, beyond Steinberg, a squad from Steinberg's platoon was hunkered down on the slope, exposed to enemy fire, but reluctant to move.

Then the enemy fire slackened, and that quickly, Steinberg was gone. Burris checked down the log; Ollie (Lang), Schoolman, Garner, Seasholtz, and Peanuts (Prinz) were all there. Beyond Peanuts, Burris wasn't sure, though a machine gunner had found a niche on the top of that log where he laid his M60. Quiet for fleeting moments.

The respite was brief. Burris next heard the ominous *thunk* of a mortar shell being dropped into a mortar tube. It was sickeningly close. The Pfc watched as Prinz, armed with an M-79 grenade launcher, cocked his head, listening to a second *thunk* from the nearby jungle, then popped up and let fly with his thump gun. "Peanuts took that mortar out with one shot from his M-79. I heard a plop from his position down to my right, and that was all we heard from that mortar."[101]

Peanuts disappeared. "Where's Peanuts?" Garner was asking. Sergeant Schoolman looked around. "Where's Peanuts?" Schoolman shouted as the firing escalated. Someone answered that Langston had called him over to the right flank. Langston needed a good man with the M-79, and everyone knew "Peanuts" was the best.

Ollie Lang saw something. "It's a gook!" everyone shouted and opened up with full automatic M16 fire (and that M60 as well) that shredded the jungle before them but somehow missed the guerilla.

A point-blank fusillade began to chop up the log. No one from the 3rd Platoon dared to raise his head. Burris decided that the enemy soldier sighted by Lang was sent forward to pinpoint the Americans' position. "Now they know where we are," he thought to himself.

And that is when the bottom dropped out.

..

Farther back in the perimeter, the rattle of gunfire and the mortar explosions rocketed into a roar that signaled the first brutal seconds of the renewed engagement. These were moments when the company's command structure was severely crippled. Captain Nolen and veteran non-coms were wounded.

Other soldiers abandoned their weapons and began frantically shrinking into the earth in a futile attempt to avoid the suddenly lethal airspace above them. The realization that the Americans needed to escape was heightened because the men recognized that they were surrounded.

Nolen and his XO, Lieutenant Ken Alderson, quickly conferred about the situation (this was before Nolen was wounded). Alderson told Nolen that the company needed to break out of the tightening noose. Nolen's response was, "we gotta get out of here," instructing Alderson to take two squads from the 1st and 2nd platoons and punch through the VC lines in the 1st Platoon's area. That was the area that seemed to be under the least amount of fire at the time.

With the company busted up, the enemy munitions knifing through the perimeter, Alderson and his radio operator low ran in the general direction of 1st Platoon. As Alderson began this run, he watched in horror as a mortar round burst about six feet from him, sending deadly shrapnel into the air. A Vietnamese national policeman who was attached to the company was blasted to the ground by the explosion. Luckily the shrapnel slapped broadside against his back. Rather than the jagged edges slicing through him, he was knocked down by the flat of the shrapnel.

No American artillery answered the guerilla barrage. General DePuy later told Lieutenant Kroah that he (DePuy) had initially withheld supporting fire after the first American shells had been misdirected and rained down on Charlie Company's position. Lieutenant Fox, the Forward Observer, radioed to the battery supporting the Americans and asked for fire. The battery crew told Fox that the guns were running low on shells.

Fox screamed back into the radio, "Haven't you ever heard of a fucking resupply!" Alderson, the Vietnamese policeman, and the other soldiers had to endure the mortar attack without support.

However, Alderson's responsibilities propelled him to move again. He had to keep moving to get to 1st Platoon. So, once again, he started off. Moving forward, Alderson plunged for the dirt as the fire zeroed in on him. The officer's RTO, Thomas C. Bash, was right beside him in the maneuver. The lieutenant had his face turned toward the GI when he saw a puff of dust geyser up from Bash's helmet. The radioman's head went down, the force of the shot knocking his face down into the ground. Alderson was sure his RTO had taken a headshot. Alderson gripped Bash by the collar and rolled him over.

"What's wrong," asked Bash. The bullet had bitten but failed to penetrate the helmet.

The officer and the RTO made it to the 1st Platoon and informed Sergeant Sutterfield of the orders for a breakout. The Platoon Sergeant ordered his weapons squad sergeant, Pete Faberski, to ready 2nd Squad and make the attempt. Dour-faced Faberski instructed the 2nd Squad to "saddle up," and ordered the men forward immediately.

In the confusion of battle, Faberski did not realize that Alderson was along for the assault. Years later, Alderson could not recall the names of the men in the assault. Roger Harris, Platoon Sergeant Sutterfield's radioman, participated in the attack after Sutterfield assigned him to Faberski. Harris remembers that 1st Platoon's Lieutenant DeVoe Smith was in on the charge. 2nd Squad, 1st Platoon bounded forward, and from the bushes to their front sprang a torrent of lead. The point man made a few steps before being hit. The other men flattened on the jungle floor as the wounded man cried out for a medic.

It was an agonizing moment of clarity for the 2nd Squad, 1st Platoon; they were not going anywhere, not forward into that kill zone to retrieve their stricken comrade, and not out of the perimeter.

The incoming fire roared. It was one-sided. 1st Platoon was getting nailed to the ground and not fighting back. Alderson saw two men go down when the assault faltered. He tried to make himself as flat as possible as the incoming bullets rained in. His helmet was blasted from his head by a sniper round, but he was unhurt. He saw that the big antenna on Bash's radio was attracting enemy fire, so he instructed his RTO to ditch the radio. Bash extrapolated on the order and hightailed it toward the command post. Alderson, isolated in an inferno, and without a way to communicate, retreated in search of his commander.

Hemmed in by the enemy fire, including automatic weapons fire, Sergeant Faberski slowly picked his way backward. He had to report to Sutterfield. Faberski noted that the volume of fire was rising to impossible levels even as he crawled toward Sutterfield. His progress seemed painfully slow; he could not seem to get away from the zipping bullets just above his head. Finally, he found Sutterfield. Simultaneously First Sergeant Takeguchi – the company's First Sergeant who never went on field operations, except for this one—came slithering up on his belly to ask, "What's going on? Can we make it out?"

Saving Sutterfield and Faberski the bother of answering, the trees around the trio began splintering from the heavy slugs of a .51 caliber hammering into the tree trunks, blowing off chunks of wood. Takeguchi and Sutterfield were hit by small arms fire at the same moment. Sutterfield's wound was a painful bullet hole through the left wrist. Though not immediately life-threatening, the wound did bust up the arm enough to make it useless and take Sutterfield out of the battle. Takeguchi was hit in the shoulder with a sniper's bullet that passed through, which meant the unit lost another senior NCO.

Sutterfield calmly bandaged his wrist, looked over to Faberski, and said, "Pete, you're in charge."

That worried Faberski. It was not being placed in charge that worried Faberski, but that Sutterfield had called him by his given name as opposed to the nickname "Hoss." It was a sobering moment.

..

By the time Sutterfield and Takeguchi had been wounded, Captain Nolen had also been hit. The day's work was Nolen's first encounter with combat. In the initial stages of the fighting, he had been able to rely on his platoon leaders to bring the company through the firefight. Once the battle had reignited and the platoons were isolated, with the platoon leaders concerned for their men and not with overall tactics, Nolen's only thought seemed to be to get his neck out of the vice. Besides sending Alderson off to lead a breakout attempt, he told Dave Peters, his radio operator, to move out. Peters looked around at the trees being splintered by the machine gun shells, listened to the bullets gnawing through the perimeter, and cringed as the mortars fell from the sky and thought, "Move out where?" Despite the order to Peters, Nolen did not attempt to move, so Peters and a medic laid down next to Nolen, who had sought refuge behind a log.

One mortar shell exploded near the trio. Peters felt a searing pain in his thigh. Nolen was next to him, screaming, "Medic! I'm hit." The cries were useless; the medic on the other side of Peters had taken shrapnel in the side. He was in no condition to doctor anyone. The medic was panicky, unable to dress the wound. Peters broke with procedure, took out his bandage, and patched up the medic. Next, the RTO turned to Nolen. The fight was out of the captain. He had been hit in the buttocks by sniper fire. For the remainder of the fight, Nolen would sporadically give orders, but he never controlled the company after being hit.*

The company had lost its commanding officer and critical NCOs in the first moments of this new crisis. Besides Nolen's loss, there was the wounding of Takeguchi and 1st Platoon's Hugh Sutterfield—two veteran sergeants who could have brought some experience to the fight. Up front in the 3rd Platoon's area, Lieutenant Kroah could not locate his platoon sergeant to coordinate defense, while the 4th Platoon's lieutenant, Steinberg, had already been wounded, and the platoon sergeant, Staff Sergeant Bozy Gerald, was pinned down under the galling fire of a machine gun. In the 1st Platoon's area, Lieutenant Smith DeVoe and Sergeant Faberski were still reeling from the aborted breakout attempt while Alderson was temporarily out of touch with other commanders. It was the company in freefall.

..

With Captain Nolen essentially incapacitated, Alderson missing, and assumed dead, Lieutenant Libs of 2nd Platoon decided that another charge had to be made to pierce the "kill sack" holding C Company. Libs had the most faith in his friend Lieutenant Kroah. He got Kroah on the radio.

"We've got to break out of this perimeter," Libs told Kroah.

Yards from several .30 caliber machine guns that were chewing up the landscape, Kroah wondered if Libs understood what he was asking of him. However, all Kroah said over the radio was, "Johnny, I'll try."

Kroah called out to a squad leader, Staff Sergeant Philip Alonso Jones of Washington D.C., "Get up and get your men moving. Try to get the hell out of here."

Jones looked at Kroah as if the lieutenant was "one crazy fool." Despite misgivings, Jones made an effort to move, getting up on one knee. Jones was a gregarious NCO who talked proudly of his Ford Mustang and of the bottle of Wild Turkey whiskey he was going to buy the first thing when he made it back home. As soon as Jones levered himself up on that one knee, he was hit squarely in the chest. He fell over dead. Jones was twenty-seven.

"There's just no way," Kroah radioed Libs.

Somehow Sergeant Langston, known as the "Round Man" for his barrel-like physique, positioned on 3rd Platoon's right flank, got word of the breakout order. Langston, who had managed to produce a can of beer to share with friends in the middle of a battlefield, was determined to make the assault. The "Roundman," 3rd platoon's Napoleon-sized hurricane. A photo taken during the division's debarkation in June of 1965 that eventually found its way into the 2nd Brigade's yearbook shows Langston lugging a box of C rations and grimacing under the weight of the load. Langston's teeth are clenched, his muscles taunt, his eyes two black slits with bushy eyebrows shading them. The pose could have easily portrayed the Sergeant when he "had the ass." Langston was twenty-six—when he walked that chow off the *Gordon*—and another genuine article married-to-the-Army, no-chickenshit-tolerating non-com. Because of his height (he was "short" according to Company C men of average height) and a tendency to carry too much weight around his middle, he got the nickname "Roundman." That label may have prompted him to quickly challenge anyone seeming to test his authority. He would jump into a soldier's shit pronto, and as he blew his bottom lip in and out with a "ppppptttttt" sound—a tick that spelled trouble for the unfortunate trooper that got him to that level of pique—he would work a pencil from eraser to lead point, crawling the tips of his fingers up the pencil shaft until he reached the top, then flipping it and beginning again. He was a skirt-chasing Arkansan who you could be certain would have a fifth of whiskey in his hand when he searched out his friend Staff Sergeant Sutterfield. Langston, Sutterfield, and Faberski formed a troika of friends, each ramrodding a Charlie Company platoon that July day in 1965 when the photo of Langston was taken. The three had been friends since Faberski had arrived at Ft. Riley.

For the assault, Langston grabbed feisty Randall "Peanuts" Prinz and newbie Pfc David A. Hammett of Chicago. There were two or three others. Langston (The Round Man was more stout than fat) vaulted up and led these men in a dash directly toward the enemy lines.[102]

Dan Kirby watched the assault, a melancholy rather than heroic charge because the attempt seemed to progress in slow motion to the frightened Kirby. The men could not move fast enough. "I didn't see any come back."

Langston and his men were caught in an enfilading fire from their right. Hammett went down. Peanuts went down. Langston staggered and fell but remained alive. The remaining men fell to the ground all around Langston. They were not dead but immobilized.

Kroah was unaware of Langston's predicament, not knowing even that Langston had tried a breakout. However, he was aware of Sergeant Richard Manley, the Korean War veteran with a reputation for toughness and know-how. As the guerillas began firing mortars through the perimeter, Manley had "lost it." The shells were plastering the area from above as the .30 caliber and the various small arms fire poured in from every direction. The combination proved too much for Manley. He bolted from his position, screaming that everyone was going to die.

The out-of-control sergeant made it as far as 1st Platoon's area where his bellowing attracted Pfc Milton Lader's attention. Lader, his chin in the dirt, respected Manley and felt sure that he had the wherewithal to keep men safe. Lader had seen Manley maneuver men coolly while under fire. And now Manley had lost it. Lader watched Manley's hysteria for a moment and then was stunned as shrapnel from a mortar round sliced through the side of Manley's head. The sergeant fell forward as if to land face down, but his face stared up toward the sky after his body hit the ground. Manley's face had been sliced off and fell next to his lifeless body.

Losing Manley was a blow. The day was turning ugly fast. It reminded Lader of another day back in September of '65 that had involved Manley and a bad turn of events. During Operation PLUMBOB, a battalion-sized search and destroy mission near Tân Uyên, the company commander at the time, Captain Robert Canady, received a request from Division HQ for a REMF$^\pm$ to accompany the unit on its mission. The company grunts believed that the REMF, a captain, was hunting a wholesale CIB**, a quick fix to the hazards of duty in the rear—said hazards amounting to not glomming onto proof of combat experience, a prerequisite for upward mobility in the officer ranks.

The REMF was among the men of Charlie Company along the Song Dong Nai (Dong Nai River) in mid-September. The company had traveled by truck, then boat, as they were brought to their operational area. For Pfc Lader, the day was clear, and the duty easy. The company rousted a hamlet, turning up nothing. Moving across the Dong Nai, Lader was counting this day as a breeze. Tramp a few rice paddies, then back in, another search-no-destroy.

Across the river lay a sea of paddy land cut through with tree-lined ditches bordered by steep-sided berms. The company chose to hike along one of those berms.

The first shot dropped the REMF, though no one realized he was hit in the immediate aftermath of the shot because the entire company had flattened out in the muddy paddy water. It was only as the GIs lifted their soggy heads that they realized that the captain had failed to do the same. Then they snapped that he was hit.

"He was out of it…dead. The medics brought that guy back to life."

What Lader saw of the resuscitation of the REMF came from fish/leech/rice root level, because he, like the rest of Charlie Company was treading water in a rice paddy while the enemy blanketed the air with deadly metal just over their heads. "We were down low, along the banks of a ditch that cut through [the rice paddy]. They needed someone to get up in the tree [the tree was growing out of the ditch]."

Confusion swallowed the first few moments of the firefight. A machine gun crew was blazing away indiscriminately, while the medics worked over the REMF, radio men called for an evac chopper, and the rest of the company edged their weapons over the crown of the berm to lay down defensive fire. This encounter had veered away from the typical Charlie Company action; it was more than a sniper out to zap a GI. The enemy wanted a higher score. The continuing fire was unusual and confusing – a situation that confounded efforts to locate the enemy. Klaus Grill, Captain Canady's driver, even worried that the American soldiers' randomly aimed but continual shooting risked burning through the Company's ammo. Sergeant Manley, unfazed in this tight spot, reacted with that cool professionalism that was reassuring to the younger men – which is not to say he didn't raise his voice when he ordered Lader up that convenient tree.

Lader shimmied up the tree. Bullets snapped by but the VC didn't seem to pay him any special attention. In a heartbeat —

that particular heartbeat that can last an eternity but is over in a flash—the GI scanned the rice paddy. In the next instant, he spotted the enemy behind the dike at the far end of the paddy. "I can see'em," Lader shouted down to Manley at the same time he propped his M14 against a limb and opened up on the dike. Training kicked in. He was running on automatic. He laid down a base of fire.

That got the bad guys' attention. Limbs exploded all around Lader's perch. Steel hornets were buzzing by Lader's head. "I didn't have shit up there but me," and a bunch of VC bullets. "Ain't no way I'm staying up that tree." He jumped through a hail of gunfire to splash into the ditch. He then joined the rest of the platoon in sticking the barrel of his rifle over the top of that ditch and firing.

With the company then shooting in the right direction the VC decided that one wounded American captain was enough of a tally after all and they vanished into the bush. The wounded captain was medevacked out and Lader's easy day had become the day he realized that Vietnam wasn't a lark. Months later, with Manley's macabre death, somehow Lader realized April 11 was going to be much worse than when he was out on a limb in September.

..

Manley fell dead and the enemy chose that moment to attack. Along the 3rd and 4th Platoons' sectors, the guerillas jolted from the trenches to attempt to crack the American lines. Simultaneously, snipers in the trees sprayed Charlie Company with a shower of bullets to cover the charge. The attackers surged forward but ebbed against the concerted efforts of the desperate men of 3rd and 4th platoons.[103]

Battered by that killing wave was Spec 4 Edward (Eddie) George of Myrtle Creek, Oregon, a newbie who had been in

Vietnam for a month. He steadied himself and began purposefully wielding his M79 grenade launcher to kill the enemy. The Vietcong pressed in on the 4th Platoon's positions. George remained cool, letting a grenade fly when he saw Vietcong bunching or where the guerillas were threatening a breakthrough.[104‡]

Elsewhere in the 4th Platoon's area, Lieutenant Steinberg reacted to the assault with the aplomb of a MacArthur or a Patton. The Army citation for his Distinguished Service Cross states that Steinberg "...moved from position to position...fighting savagely to beat back the...insurgents which closed in at pointblank range."[105] 4th Platoon only had twelve effectives by this time. Steinberg was severely hurt, and many of the twelve remaining men were wounded. As the survivors beat back the assault, the firing to the 4th Platoon's front slackened.

In the 3rd Platoon's sector, halting the enemy's attack was also a close-run thing. As the guerillas charged the 3rd Platoon, Kroah was hit in the back of the neck by a grenade fragment. The lieutenant spotted tracers bursting forth from the bushes to his front and left. He figured it for a machine gun. He took careful aim and let the M16 buck on automatic. There were no more tracers from that particular bush.

Then Kroah received his second wound of the day. He was hit in the shoulder, with the bullet scoring his flesh as it dug a bloody trench down his back.

3rd Platoon was disintegrating. Langston was out beyond the perimeter. Kroah was out of commission. Sergeant Jones was dead. Sergeant Navarro, another squad leader, was wounded by the earlier friendly fire and moved to the CP area. Sergeant Schoolman was all that remained of the 3rd Platoon's command structure, and he was minutes away from going down himself.

The enemy's covering fire was so unremitting that Sergeant Langston, pinned beyond the perimeter with his detachment, could only reposition his wounded men to defend against the onslaught. The enemy came on. A VC materialized among the injured Americans. Langston grappled with the guerilla. Other Vietcong poured forward. As Langston fought his attacker, an enemy machine gun supporting the attack swung its killing arc toward the struggling soldiers. Langston and the guerilla he was fighting fell instantly. The other men in the detachment were killed or dying.[106]

Men fought as individuals with no thought of tactics or orders. They fired when they could. They buried their heads when they could. They clung to their sanity in moments that were insane. And they died.

The Vietcong came on. One man's acts saved the 3rd Platoon's line from being ruptured. Pfc Deane Van Dyke, operating that M60 machine gun propped up on the big log, unleashed a killing spray of machine-gun fire into the ranks of charging guerillas. Van Dyke's Bronze Star citation reads in part, "During the initial assault, Private First Class Van Dyke effectively placed heavy volumes of fire on Vietcong snipers who were inflicting numerous casualties on the American forces. The Vietcong singled out his machine gun position, and...Van Dyke was wounded during their fierce concentration of fire on his area."[107] Van Dyke continued to handle his gun until the enemy was driven off.§

Spec 4 Howard Blevins, the Burnsville, North Carolinian from the communications detail who had ventured into the 3rd Platoon's area to deliver needed ammunition, now showed up at Lieutenant Kroah's side.

"I've got no ammo and I went to the machine gun and the gunner's dead and they [the VC] have stolen the gun!" Blevins shouted.§§

Then Kroah watched in horror as a sniper "ripped him up the back. Three rounds." Blevins eyes glazed over even before he fell. The quiet twenty-one-year-old died because he had been concerned for friends in another unit [3rd Platoon] and so had left the relative safety of his position for the much more exposed 3rd Platoon sector.

Sergeant Schoolman heard that Langston and others were out in front of the lines. He called for volunteers to go and retrieve their friends. Rugged Sergeant Ronald Seasholtz spoke up. The wounded Van Dyke volunteered. Pfc John "Ollie" Lang said he would go: "I remember looking at…the rest of my squad as I buckled up my chin strap.

I told them to cover me as I got up. I remember that they gave me a funny look like they were saying goodbye. I felt scared and weird. They started shooting, and we went out."

The rescuers bolted into the deadly no man's land. They did not get far before Seasholtz went down with a gut wound. The bullets were everywhere. Van Dyke was hit again. Lang rushed to Seasholtz, grabbed him, and retreated while firing.

Though wounded twice, Van Dyke managed to drag a body back to the perimeter. Lang left the wounded Seasholtz with Spec 4 Richard Garner and cried, "I'm going out to get the rest, cover me!" Both Lang and Van Dyke ventured beyond the perimeter to rescue other platoon members. Lang picked up Langston's lifeless body, and Van Dyke retrieved another. Then machine-gun bullets blasted Van Dyke in the side. He would not be going out again.

Lang did go out again. He had lost his helmet, pack, and ammunition. He was in a frenzy. He scooped up some equipment from the bloody ground where Langston had laid.

The Pfc felt a burning sensation on his right foot. He looked down to see most of the front of his boot blown off.

Lang saw a massive gash on his naked calf. The bone was exposed. Remarkably he could still walk on the injured leg.

The sight of the wound infuriated Lang. He had never been shot before! He wanted blood for blood. He snatched up some ammo from another soldier and made his way back toward the enemy. "I shot everyone I could see." He also helped more wounded toward the perimeter, but the perimeter was no longer there.

Sergeant Schoolman's squad was coming under withering fire, and when Burris pointed out that the 4th Platoon squad that had tied in on the left flank had disappeared, the sergeant ordered the remainder of the men to pull back. This contraction of the perimeter was happening all along the company line. The pressure from the Vietcong was so relentless that the healthy men were forced back on themselves. Unfortunately, this meant men like Kroah, his radio man Conway, and the wounded medic were left outside the perimeter. Spec 4 Richard Garner refused to leave the dying Sergeant Seasholtz and so was separated from his squad. Wes Carpenter was a few yards away, crawling from rifleman to rifleman administering rudimentary first aid or bringing his buddies weapons and ammo. Pfc Lang was able to crawl up the slight slope to locate some of the 3rd Platoon. And, though no one knew it at the time, Hammett and Prinz, wounded out in the original no man's land, were not dead, but they were now hopelessly beyond reach in the maw that seemed to be swallowing all of Charlie Company.

Langston had led men into the teeth of the enemy's guns and died there. Sergeant Seasholtz and Van Dyke were mortally wounded in the attempt to rescue Langston and the other men wounded outside the perimeter. Seasholtz's life ebbed away on the battlefield with his friend Spec 4 Richard Garner at his side.

Van Dyke was discovered alive on the battlefield the next day and evacuated, lingering for weeks in a military hospital, dying on the day he was to be transferred to a United States hospital. John Lang repeatedly risked his life to retrieve his comrades' bodies while unleashing his fiery response to the encroaching enemy. And when Lang attempted to gain the safety of the company perimeter, he found that the perimeter was not where he had left it!

..

Private Emmett Mays, a "ner-do-well" who was habitually bumming money from other platoon members, sought direction from the wounded Lieutenant Kroah. A grenade rolled to the officer's feet. Mays jumped between the grenade and Kroah, absorbing the blast with his body. Kroah was unclear whether Mays was simply seeking the ground's safety at Kroah's feet or shielding his commander, but Mays died either way. Kroah chooses to believe it was self-sacrifice. Then a fire team leader dove across Kroah's legs and shouted that his men were running out of ammunition. Before Kroah could respond, the team leader had been shot dead. Trapped in this nightmare where his men sought him out only to be killed for the effort, Kroah realized he had lost control of his platoon.

At that time, Kroah felt as if his descent into chaos had reached bottom. He had been hit a third time—this wound was the result of grenade fragments tearing into his back. The enemy had spotted the radio's antennae on RTO Conway's back. The enemy had a specific target to concentrate on, so they blasted the area around Kroah. The lieutenant was hit in the calf and ankle. Wounds number four and five. The new-guy medic, already frozen with fear, was shot in the back.

Bullets clipped the cord on Conway's radio. Kroah, in a repeat of Alderson's scene with his radioman, saw a puff of smoke rise from the RTO's helmet. Conway grabbed the helmet and ripped it off. There was no blood on the soldier's head. The bullet had penetrated the helmet, circled the RTO's head, and exited the back without hitting him.

"Damn, I thought I'd been hit."

Immediately after Conway spoke, a bullet slammed through the radio and hit him in the back. Then the radioman's shoulder was perforated with a round from a sniper.

"Help me. Help me," Conway yelled at Kroah. The RTO frantically reminded the wounded Kroah that a family was waiting for him back in Alabama. "I don't want to die here."

"Shut the fuck up," commanded the lieutenant, who had his own family to worry about and who had no intention of dying in Vietnam. Kroah commanded Conway to stay quiet and still.[108]

..

The Vietcong were not so easily vexed in their attempts to overrun the Americans. They had struck both the 3rd and 4th platoon's sectors and been driven off—barely driven off. The enemy commander must have surreptitiously surveyed the battered, bloody ground in the 4th Platoon's area and decided on another push because a second assault rushed toward the 4th Platoon.

The guerillas rallied, regrouped, and sprang forth again, pounding 4th Platoon's sector with the combined weight of a .51 caliber machine gun and all the small arms fire that could be concentrated on the spot. Mortars continued their tattoo across the platoon's position. Fortunately, the American battery supporting Charlie Company had finally roared into life. They inundated the enemy front lines with high explosives. The enemy mortars were silenced, and the regrouped guerillas shattered. The charge came on, but it was weak and soon fell apart.

The twelve remaining men of the 4th Platoon braced themselves for the assault. Pfc George, the grenadier who had broken up pockets of guerillas in the first assault, readied his weapon to defend against the next assault. He placed his shots with deadly accuracy, even as the insurgents focused on him and his deadly grenade launcher. He did not falter despite the incoming rounds until a bullet found its mark and killed him.[109]

The guerillas fell back. Let the .51 caliber machine gun do its work. Possibly Lieutenant Steinberg realized that the .51 would decimate his unit; possibly, as his citation reads, Steinberg realized that he was outnumbered and a charge might surprise the enemy.[110] Perhaps it was just a Steinberg move, hare-brained but impossibly brave.

The lieutenant ordered his men to take out the .51 with an attack. Steinberg rose and, hurling grenades as he went, ran directly toward the machine gun. Some men followed while others shot into the trees in an attempt to stop the snipers. Spec 4 Charles D. Oglesby, and Sergeant William Causey, chased behind Steinberg. A grenade burst stopped Oglesby. Causey was killed instantly when a slug from the .51 tore into him. Others ran to fill the fallen's places. Steinberg was hit repeatedly but continued to throw grenades until he dropped from the combined wounds. Staff Sergeant Ralph Coleman and Pfc Leroy Love were hurling grenades as well when Coleman was shot down. These men and others who followed Steinberg were able to silence the .51 before retreating to the line.[111]

Yards north of where Steinberg lay, Marty Kroah was shocked to hear a shout from Steinberg. From *Mud Soldiers*, author George Wilson relates that Steinberg called for help.

"George, I can't help you. I've been hit five times." Kroah replied.

Steinberg shouted again. "I've been hit seven."

"Always the bullshitter, huh, George?"

4th Platoon's commander responded, "No bullshit, man."

George Wilson then writes, "And it wasn't. Steinberg died with those words."[112]

It had been barely two hours since Lieutenant DeVoe of 1st Platoon had thought the fight was over. Just an hour and a half since the Air Force Huskies had been driven from the skies above the evacuation area. It had been mere minutes since the perimeter contracted under the Vietcong pressure. Yet, to each man of Company C, it had been an eternity since they had slipped over the precipice.

---

*Captain Nolen's other RTO, Gilbert Delao, responsible for internal Company communications, remembers going to Nolen to patch him up with his bandage. Nolen waved Delao off, saying, "Save it, you may need it yourself." This sobering advice indicated to Delao how bad the situation had become.

± (R)ear (E)chelon (M)other (F)ucker

** (C)ombat(I)nfantry(B)adge

‡ I've placed Edward (Eddie) George in the 4th platoon's area during the battle because the description of his actions in his citation for the Bronze Star is consistent with him being in that part of the battlefield. Eddie's platoon is unknown, though the 2nd platoon can be eliminated (The 2nd platoon lost only one man killed on April 11, 1966) while none of the survivors of the 1st or 3rd platoon recall him. No one I interviewed from the 4th platoon remembers Eddie either, but due to the Bronze Star award text, I am comfortable placing him in the 4th platoon.

§I've located Deane Van Dyke, Jr. in the 3rd platoon on the evidence of a letter written by a survivor after the battle. I quote, "Lt. Kroah, Sgt. Schoolman, Garner, Klopfer, *Van Dyke*, [italics added] Whiteside are in the hospital. They all got shot two and three times."

§§Blevins had stumbled upon the big log where Van Dyke and so many of the 3rd platoon members had sought refuge. Unfortunately for Blevins, this was after the VC push that resulted in Van Dyke's mortal wounding and the platoon's retreat related later in the chapter. The guerillas had moved forward and taken Van Dyke's abandoned machine gun.

Photos

Medal of Honor Recipient
Sgt. James R. Robinson, Jr.
Courtesy of
Colonel Robert R. McCormick
Research Center
First Division Museum at Cantigny Park

Particular Bravery: The Battle of Xa Cam My And The Death of a Grunt Company

Medal of Honor Recipient
A1C William H. Pitsenbarger
Courtesy of
Colonel Robert R. McCormick
Research Center
First Division Museum at Cantigny Park

Particular Bravery: The Battle of Xa Cam My And The Death of a Grunt Company

"the Barber SAID, NEXt!"
Paid Consideration
The Associated Press

Chapter Five:
"A Serious Blow"

"Whenever the VC thought they saw an advantage, they would precipitate a fight...A VC battalion surrounded an American company and before reinforcements could intervene, killed 48 Americans. Although VC losses were double that, it was still *a serious blow* for such a small force."

General William Westmoreland, A Soldier Reports, p. 232. (italics added to the text)

Pfc Ted Piner of Columbia, Mississippi, was a dead shot. His skills with a rifle were such that he had been a member of a classified team of marksmen testing the M16 back in the states. The testing was so secretive that the team had to retrieve their locked-away and covered rifles each day from the armory so that they could test them far from prying eyes, rapid-firing the rifles to judge their durability and accuracy, then returning the weapons to an officer who oversaw storage of the classified rifles. Because he participated in the testing, Piner knew the M16 as well as anyone in the U.S. Army. Despite this knowledge, when Piner arrived in Vietnam in March 1966, he was handed an M14, a weapon he had not been trained to use.

Some NCO had poked an M14 into Piner's hands "just in case," after the jet bringing Piner to Vietnam had approached Tan Son Nhut airfield at a stomach-churning pitch. The airbase was under threat of attack. By the time the newbies were hustled into a truck the threat was over. The truck rattled them to a dilapidated building where they were crammed into a dingy room that had walls peppered with bullet holes.

"What the hell have I gotten myself into?" wondered Piner.

The Mississippian had gotten himself into some more target practice, for Piner arrived in the company at approximately the same time as Captain Ramon Padilla — Charlie Company's commanding officer preceding Captain Nolen—and Padilla wanted everyone proficient with the M14 and every other weapon the unit was equipped with at the time. By his second day with the company, Piner was blazing away with an M14 while other grunts were taking target practice with .45 pistols and blooping out grenades with the M79 grenade launcher. Once the soldier felt reasonably sure that he could handle the M14 the Army took that weapon away from the company and supplied them with M16s. The Army also replaced the by-the-book Padilla with the religious Nolen though Padilla had been with the Company for only one month. On this April afternoon, Piner was on his second rifle, second commander, and his second calendar month in Vietnam.

Piner had taken cover when the shooting started. Pfc Edward Riley – the same gregarious soldier who earlier in the operation had gone out of his way to befriend the friendless new medic Dave Marchetti—told Piner to stay close, listen to him. The first minutes of the renewed fight had washed around Piner and Riley without materially affecting them. Around 5:00 P.M. Piner heard someone, possibly Buck Sergeant John D. Fulford, lament, "Third Platoon's gone." Next, Piner made out Lieutenant Libs' voice as he cajoled his men, "We've got to attack. Break out."

It was the 2nd Platoon's turn to try to break the stranglehold on the company. Libs called Sergeant Fulford over to his side. Fulford had been put in charge of a squad after Sergeant Passmore had been evacuated on a helicopter. Libs ordered Fulford to gather his men and break out of the encirclement. Piner was the second GI behind the point: Pfc Reilly.

Reilly dashed forward. Behind Reilly came Piner, Phil Hall, and others, all blazing away. Then the enemy opened up. A wall of lead slammed into Reilly. Reilly's head snapped back, blood painted the air, and the point man went down clutching at a crucifix around his neck.

Everyone else went down to stay alive. Grenades burst, but the blasts were up and out so that the GIs flat on the ground were relatively safe. Some of the men attempted to scramble forward as if they were continuing the charge at worm level. This half-hearted crawl ended quickly. There were too many tracers in the air, too much shrapnel finding its mark—Pfc Doug Landry felt the burn of grenade fragments pierce his backside – for the assault to continue. A grenade landed at Piner's side.

The explosion lifted Piner into the air. He was knocked unconscious.

The men were now scrambling *back* toward some semblance of safety—moving away from the guerillas. Lieutenant Libs was shouting for the men to retreat. Landry was moving despite his wound, but Piner was out cold. Sergeant Fulford heard his lieutenant scream, "You come out," and Fulford did not hesitate to follow that order. He managed to hug the ground as he made his way back to Libs, then moved on to man a machine gun after the gunner was hit or simply disappeared.

Phil Hall wanted to get back to the perimeter after a grenade had blasted two pieces of shrapnel into his right arm. Initially, Hall had been stunned by the grenade, his vision blurred and turned the world purple around him; still, the wounds did not stop him from moving, but the voice of another American did halt Hall's retreat. The same grenade that had wounded Hall had also torn into another trooper near him. Pfc Jackie K. Lancaster plaintively asked Hall if he [Hall] could help him back to the perimeter. Hall bulled on elbows and knees to the wounded Lancaster. For a moment, they appeared to be wrestling as Lancaster heaved himself onto Hall's back, and then both soldiers began a painful, slow crawl toward the 2nd Platoon. Hall and Lancaster reached a big log blown down by the artillery. With all the artillery chopping down the jungle, blasted trees were laying helter-skelter all around the perimeter. The log represented potential cover if the two men could get over it to the far side. However, Hall did not want to present a target for the enemy and struggling with the wounded Lancaster to get him over that log would make a huge bull's eye. Hall asked Lancaster if he could get over the log by himself. Lancaster nodded. Hall was over quickly and moving on when he looked back a final time to see Lancaster clear the log. Hall scrambled to the perimeter and took up a position next to Spec 4 John Noyce at one of the platoon's machine guns.

One 2nd Platoon soldier could not abide the thought of Reilly's body lying outside the perimeter under the guerillas' guns, while another trooper worried about the discarded weapons outside the perimeter. Specialist 4 Israel Pacheco, in Vietnam about two weeks—one of the green GIs whose combat-savvy Sergeants Sutterfield and Langston had been fretting over that morning—waited for a slackening of gunfire then made his move. He scrambled in a fast crawl to Reilly's body and, gripping it tightly, attempted to drag it back to the perimeter. The fire immediately intensified, and Pacheco had to be satisfied with getting himself away from the Vietcong guns.

At about the same time that Pacheco was retrieving Reilly's body, Pfc James C. West plunged over the log shielding so many of 2nd Platoon's men and began a sweep of the area to snatch up the rifles dropped by the retreating Americans. It was a scene that was repeated throughout the company perimeter: men like John Lang of 3rd Platoon, James Robinson of 1st Platoon, and there before the sheltering log, James C. West, risking their lives to save weapons. Arms loaded down with rifles; West made it back to the perimeter.

The assault had been stymied. However, with the 2nd Platoon's energy spent, they could only hold on, though the enemy was so close GIs said they could hear the VC tubing mortars—the mortars sliding down the tube. Lieutenant Libs sought to organize his men. He moved among those he felt needed added assurance. He would position a nervous grunt outward, showing the soldier a field of fire. Libs would say, "If you see someone, you kill 'em." Pfc John W. Watkins, attached to the company just over two weeks earlier, blurted out, "What if it's an American?" Libs said, "You kill 'em." The lieutenant knew no American would be out there.

As for Watkins, he was a sharpshooter and confident he could nail anything stupid enough to stumble into his line of sight. Born to a tobacco farmer in Tennessee, Watkins was one of six children who grew up working on the land. He enjoyed that work or found it necessary enough that he had dropped out of high school to remain on the farm to help his father with the tobacco, hogs, corn, and anything else that might bring a nickel. Two older brothers had found work beyond the confines of the farm and Watkins was his father's sole help. Watkins had received three deferments from military service on the strength of his father's needs. However, when the 3rd deferment was granted, it did not sit well with the young farmer. He told his father that he wanted to go. Watkins told his family not to worry, he would do his best for the country and then he would return; training, a year in 'Nam, and back to the farm. No one in the family tried to talk him out of going.[113]

"You are going to be OK," Libs told Watkins and then each of the other soldiers on the line. The officer gave the reluctant ones, the green ones, a "pop" on the top of their helmets with the palm of his hand before he moved on to the next one.

For the remainder of the battle, Watkins held his position, shooting any VC that dared cross his line of sight. The Tennessean only left the line to retrieve more ammunition. After returning to his place in the line a mortar round careened into his position. He received multiple shrapnel wounds. Watkins died holding the line.*

..

The company was barely holding on—there would be no more attempts at breaking out. There was not enough coordination for another attempt. There was no longer any communication between platoons. No one at the CP even knew that the 4th Platoon was fighting off a third assault by hurling

CS (tear gas) canisters and smoke grenades until the sickening cloud of gas was caught by the wind and blown back into the perimeter. With Nolen wounded and Alderson still isolated, the command group was tending to the wounded more than running the battle. There was precious little coordination even within platoons. Lieutenant Libs positioned his men and then worked the radio to harangue Major Bibb Underwood. Underwood was in a helicopter hovering above the battle to monitor goings-on for battalion headquarters. Libs insisted to Underwood that headquarters get reinforcements moving.

The men of the 2nd Platoon, in small groups, or more often by themselves, fought on. Some did not even fight but simply covered their heads and waited to die while everyone listened to the anguished cries of wounded soldiers all around them.

When Libs' radio fizzled out, the lieutenant looked around, saw Phil Hall, and ordered the big man to find another radio. "I've got to have a radio to call in artillery or we're dead. Find me one!"[114]

With Hall moving out in one direction, Libs ordered Douglas Landry to head in the other direction to scrounge a radio as well. Landry quickly found a dead RTO and wrenched the radio off the corpse. Moving back towards Libs' location, a .30 caliber opened up on Landry, a slug hitting him in the right ribs, shattering one of the bones. Landry pulled the radio behind him as he managed to crawl back to Libs, but Landry was done as a fighting soldier for the day.

Hall, too, had to make his way under the intense fire of machine guns and small arms fire. He picked through the dead and wounded until he came across a wounded radioman from another platoon.

"Sorry, I've got to take this," Hall told the wounded man.
"No problem."
Author George Wilson describes what happened next;

"He [the wounded RTO] was lying on his back, bleeding to death. Hall looked into his eyes and saw the hurt and puzzlement of a boy about to die…The boy tried to turn his body to make it easier for Hall to take away his radio. Hall had no way to help the dying boy. He left him on the jungle floor to die alone. His radio, set on the same frequency being used by Underwood in the chopper overhead, was soon in Libs' hands."[115]

Libs took up one radio. Lieutenant Alderson—who had returned to the CP area by this time—took up the other. When Alderson got Major Underwood on the radio, Underwood commented, "Your voice sounds funny."

Alderson replied, "Your voice would sound funny too if you were down here!" On the ground, the perimeter was coming apart. 1st Platoon was fragmented. Sergeant Sutterfield was wounded and out of the battle. Lieutenant DeVoe was struggling simply to keep himself and those immediately around him alive. Sergeant John Bradley, a 1st Platoon squad leader, had been wounded in the renewed onslaught but continued to encourage his men, telling them to pick their targets as he crawled from one to the other. Still, his wound limited his effectiveness. Sergeant Pete Faberski, the man Sutterfield had designated to take over the platoon after Sutterfield had been shot in the arm, was crawling through the blood-splattered underbrush attempting to get 1st Platoon organized. He was discovering that, for the most part, men were no longer listening to commands. Unable to get the men working in tandem, Faberski began gathering up discarded weapons and ammunition. Many men were calling for weapons now that the renewed attack's initial shock was wearing off. These same grunts had discarded their rifles and other weapons in their panic. With the attack ratcheting up they needed those weapons again, a rifle, a pistol, anything to ward off the enemy. However, many were unwilling to move even slightly to retrieve their weapons. Faberski took it upon himself to redistribute these weapons.

Moving through an artillery-blighted landscape of smashed-up trees and bomb craters—the jungle floor was now bare churned dirt—Faberski also caught the plaintive cries of the wounded. The call of "medic" seemed to come from every direction. To Faberski, it was as if he was the only man left unwounded.

Then Faberski heard Sergeant Sutterfield shouting as well. Platoon Sergeant Sutterfield, the hard-as-nails NCO who, though wounded, was still seeking to help his men. He was yelling at Faberski to find the second M60 machine gun crew and shift them more in the direction from where the enemy's .30 caliber machine guns were raking 1st Platoon's positions.

Faberski's primary responsibility was to know where the platoon's heavy weapons were situated, so he moved toward the 2nd Platoon, where he knew one of the 1st Platoon's M60 machine gun crews was supporting Libs' men. He moved with head down toward the 2nd Platoon's sector. He quickly found the weapon. The sergeant ordered the crew to pack up and get over to the 1st Platoon. The crew picked up their ammunition belts, hoisted the gun, and as soon as their movement attracted a buzz saw of lead, they froze. Faberski could not budge them.

As Faberski was attempting to jar the machine gun crew from their stupor, Sergeant James Robinson reacted to a new threat to the 1st Platoon's line. The contracting perimeter had opened a gap between the 4th Platoon's position and the 1st Platoon on their left. The enemy had discovered the hole; a small contingent of enemy soldiers was swarming into the breach. Some were firing AK47s; some were throwing grenades. They were determined to rip into that gap and create a hole that D800 could exploit to divide, isolate and eliminate Company C in detail.

Sergeant Robinson was just the type of laugh-in-the-face-of-danger character Hollywood would have chosen to plunk down in the jungle at just that spot, at just that time, with cameras whirring in the background, catching all the drama in Technicolor. He was John Wayne charging up Mt. Suribachi, Randolph Scott leading a raid on Makin Island, and Aldo Ray any place, all wrapped up into one fearless soldier. One of two former Marines in the company, Robinson was the GI who, upon joining the company back in October 1965, had told the commanding officer, "I'm going to win the Medal of Honor!" Five months later that moment had come and, as historian Steven Clay characterized the sergeant, "he was fighting with the heart of a tiger."[116] Robinson spotted the guerilla wave and hurled himself forward to claim the disputed ground.

Two "new meat" replacements, Riflemen Burt Heath and Daniel Walden, both assigned to 1st Platoon, charged behind him. Heath was a high school graduate from New Orleans who had joined the Army despite his parents' strenuous protests. Soon after arriving in Vietnam, it was apparent he was a natural with the M79 grenade launcher, so much so that months after the battle, the battalion newssheet would write a story about his ability to crank out fifteen shots from the weapon in less than a minute—with accuracy. The reporter noted that such an exploit was "...really bringing smoke." At that moment, Heath was bringing smoke on the charging VC, pelting them with explosives fired from his M79.[117]

Daniel Walden must have followed Robinson and Heath with trepidation. Or perhaps resignation, for he had told his friend, Pfc Kenneth Mize, that he would not survive Vietnam. Mize, perpetually smiling Ken Mize, had told the gangly kid from Tennessee, "Well, Danny, you need to be thinking positive." Walden had assured Mize that he had tried thinking positively, but it was clear that he would die in Vietnam despite the positive thoughts. Walden, the son of a Baptist preacher, had even informed his family, as they gathered for his send-off to Vietnam that they would not be seeing him again. He felt he would die in combat. Still, Walden hustled after Robinson and Heath.[118] That may have been the most extraordinary kind of bravery.

Along with these three members of the 1st Platoon, Pfc Thomas Steele of the 3rd Platoon found himself caught up in the defense against the oncoming guerillas. Steele had been separated from his platoon during the first Vietcong assault. He fell in with these three defenders as he followed Sergeant Robinson's orders.

Tracers shot through the chewed-up jungle. Heath's M79 sent bursts of explosive death into the enemy's ranks. Robinson's, Walden's, and Steele's M16s rang out on automatic. These four Americans cut down charging VC only to have more appear, taking the place of the fallen men.[119] There was no stopping the enemy until the fight became hand-to-hand. The two groups of men wrestled for a moment. Muzzle flashes close enough to cause powder burns. The glint of a steel blade. Finally, it was the Americans holding the gap while the bloodied Vietcong were either retreating or dead.

Two GIs hunkered down to defend their hard-earned bloody ground. The other two GIs were dead. Thomas Steele had happened upon Robinson's determined band and joined in defense of the perimeter—he had helped save the company, but now he was dead. For Daniel Walden, his doubts about his chances of survival had been prescient; he too was lying dead on the jungle floor. Robinson and Heath had some scratches, but both had come through the ordeal. Together these four Americans had stopped the enemy's concerted effort to split the company in two. Through Robinson's fearlessness, Heath's accuracy with the M79, and Walden and Steele's sacrifices, the company was saved.[120]

Robinson was not content with this small victory. He searched out other 1st Platoon troopers, encouraging them and directing their fire: "pick your targets!" The sergeant steadied the men as a gas cloud came drifting toward 1st Platoon's lines.± Though many of the men donned gas masks, Robinson could not be bothered with the gear.

Nearby, Sergeant John Bradley was ordered by someone—probably Platoon Sergeant Sutterfield—to take some men and knock out the .51 caliber machine gun that was covering that sector. As noted above, Bradley had been wounded once already but continued to work among his men. The sergeant grabbed Spec 4 Leonardus Inkelaar and Pfc Heath (who had just returned from grappling with the enemy) and directed them to follow him. The soldiers charged into the teeth of the enemy guns. They did not go far before Bradley fell with a massive wound in his thigh. Before he lost consciousness, Bradley was able to order his men back to the line.

Inkelaar and Bradley had not gotten along; the Kansan Inkelaar just seemed to rub Bradley the wrong way, while the NCO inevitably got on Inkelaar's nerves. As the tree trunks near Inkelaar shook from the huge slugs slamming into them, as the ground all about popped from the killing rounds, the Spec 4 looked out at the unconscious sergeant and knew he was going to have to rescue him. The citation for Inkelaar's Bronze Star reads in part, "Leaving his [Inkelaar's] position within the perimeter, he crawled under intense fire to administer emergency first aid to the battle casualty [Bradley]." Inkelaar stopped Bradley's bleeding as the enemy fire turned toward the two men. Inkelaar began pulling the unconscious sergeant back toward the perimeter when he was "...critically wounded in the arm by a .51 caliber machine gun bullet."[121]

The single slug ate up Inkelaar's arm from the elbow to the shoulder, shattering bone and ripping muscle. Fragments from the shell splintered off and knifed through the tissues around the collar bone and bashed against and broke three vertebrae in Inkelaar's neck. The force of the shot had also broken the Spec 4's jaw and knocked him unconscious. Both Inkelaar and Bradley lay helpless outside the perimeter.

Slightly back from the line Ken Mize had armed himself with another soldier's discarded M16. Mize had been carrying an M79 grenade launcher—useless in such close quarters—and a .45 pistol when the battle began. The GI, who had a month's experience in Vietnam, had realized that neither of those two weapons would provide much protection, so he had scrambled to find a rifle. Armed with the M16, Mize laid down on his belly and began a shooting match that he described in terms of a game of pool:

> "I could hear a lot going on... [but] as far as actually seeing the enemy face-to-face, I didn't. I saw movement. Leaves moving. Concussions of the shells blasting [through] the trees. That's what I shot at. One time I could tell that the bullets were coming into the ground from trees. I treated it like a pool shot, going from where I was at, reversing it, and seeing where the leaves and twigs were moving up to the treetops. I fired in that direction. I didn't see any bodies fall, but I think I did some good there."

Doing some good. Staying alive and killing some of the enemy soldiers. Then the battle seemed to catch up to Mize. Suddenly both his legs went numb. Since shells were tearing up the landscape all about him, the Arkansan assumed that he had been struck by shrapnel. Gingerly he reached back to feel his legs. A dirt clot so big it would have made an Arkansas diamond mine proud had smacked the back of his knees with such force that his legs had gone numb. Mize had figured himself for a big leg wound.

Realizing that he had not been hit, a new and bizarre thought surfaced in Mize's mind: guilt overwhelmed him because he had not yet been wounded! Mize had watched as his platoon sergeant, Sutterfield, had taken a bullet through the wrist. He had seen a soldier named Johnny Ivory take a single shot through both ankles. Bullets were cracking above his head, whizzing by him while mortars and artillery were churning up the real estate, and yet, other than getting a dirt shower, the enemy had not touched him.

When an AK47 round passed cleanly through the fleshy portion of his shoulder—"a sting, a thud, and a burn"—Mize felt relieved. "OK, I've got mine now," he told himself, the blood and pain absolving the GI of his guilt at the fate of his fellow soldiers.

Even Mize's wound was of the lucky sort—if any metal tearing through flesh can be considered fortunate—since it passed through his body without hitting major organs or breaking bones. Mize quickly figured out that he could continue the fight. He simply lay where he had been when shot and continued to pepper any movement in the trees.

The firing came in waves now. Along the perimeter, men listened, and some died as the enemy intensified their fire, the sheer volume of gunfire savaging the landscape. Then the fire slackened, never dying down completely, but dropping down into spats of small arms fire instead of the rising fusillade that the Americans simply could not match.

Perhaps the quieter moments came because D800's leader was assessing the damage done to his enemy. He had maneuvered one of the battalion's two .51 caliber machine guns around the 360⁰ perimeter so that it could take the rear of the company under fire. The other .51 still fronted the suffering 3rd and 4th platoons. The VC commander, Dang Ngoc Si, might have been satisfied with the placement of the .30 caliber machine guns as well, with two of them pounding 1st Platoon, another hitting 2nd Platoon, and a final two adding their punch to the .51 that was sweeping 3rd and 4th platoons.

Perhaps the guerillas needed a breather from the convulsions of battle. Maybe the battle's logistics were impossible to sustain—no group of soldiers, at least not four hundred men, could maintain such unremitting pressure. Or perhaps it was simply the natural rhythm of this particular battle, its hollow faux heartbeat measured in munitions expended and lives lost.

Whatever the cause of these momentary pauses, they did exist, a calm belying the manic horror surrounding them. In those moments, Charlie Company men raised their heads ever so slightly to take the measure of their situation. Some lost heart, seeing only impending death. Some few, though they too saw a violent end approaching, took the quiet moments to help their fellow soldiers. Wes Carpenter, his hands too swollen from injuries sustained when his rifle was blown out of his hands, and therefore unable to grip a rifle, was looking for water among the American corpses. He took the dead's canteens and then crawled to some living soldier desperate for water.

During one such pause, Sergeant Robinson lifted his head when he heard someone shout, "somebody help us," and out beyond the perimeter, he spied a medic struggling to bring a wounded GI back to the lines. Robinson did not hesitate. He bolted out of the perimeter, offering a shoulder for the wounded man to lean on as the medic, Robert "Doc" Fisher of 2nd Platoon, held the man's other arm. Five years later, Bob Fisher wrote that Robinson did the actual carrying – the medic thankfully tagged along back to the perimeter. Once more in the company's arms, Robinson went back to firing at the enemy until he heard another call for help. According to historian Andrew Woods, in his Spring, 2006 article about the battle, Robinson "noticed PFC Whittier about 20 meters away…shot in the back by a .50 caliber machine gun round." Robinson again entered the fury beyond the perimeter to retrieve a comrade. Woods described what happened next; "While ripping off Whittier's pack and carrying…"the wounded man back to the perimeter, "Robinson was shot in the arm and leg." The former Marine kept going despite the wounds and, "…pulled Whittier behind a tree."[122]

Fisher did not see Robinson's heroics because the medic was himself moving toward other wounded men. Fisher did not think of himself as a soldier. Normally, the soldiers would do the fighting; he would patch up the fighters. Yet, by this time, amid the carnage, he realized that things were well beyond normal. His faith that the men around him could handle the situation was rattled. No, by this time, his faith was gone. Faith required some rationale, no matter how convoluted and closed to outside facts. To have faith Fisher needed some system, some context in which to fit the horrific scenes swallowing the battlefield. But no system satisfied the conditions for what he had already seen on this death-shrouded ground as the Vietcong renewed their attack. That absence of cohesion, of a system, had killed his belief that the soldiers around him could handle the situation.

The downward spiraling horrors that had led up to Fisher's attempt to retrieve the wounded GI outside the perimeter—the attempted rescue that had required Fisher to call for help, the call that had attracted Sergeant Robinson's attention—had extinguished his belief that Charlie Company could handle the situation. Fisher had seen one soldier with his shoulders loaded down with machine gun ammunition, though the man was nowhere near a machine gun. The soldier just kept about the business of firing and loading his M16. Fisher moved past the man** when he heard a sickening thud. "There was almost a splashing sound as a bullet cut into bone and flesh." The force of the impact into the soldier's head was so great that Fisher, a few feet away, was splattered with blood as he turned to check on the ammunition-ladened soldier. Blood and brains temporarily blinded Fisher. When Fisher wiped away the blood, he could see that aid was not necessary. "[T]he man had been hit in the forehead...above his right eye. The bullet had traveled through and out the right side of his head, just over his ear." The exit wound was massive. Still, the dead GI gripped the trigger of his M16. At that moment, the shock, the horror, gave way to that loss of faith for Fisher. "I stared at him for a moment. I...held on to his wrist and stared at his wound." Fisher was overwhelmed with sadness. The dead soldier's best had not been good enough. Not in this nightmare land where the best-trained soldiers in the world could be alive one moment and, in the next, "...as fast as a bullet can travel..." be gone. Fisher could not help but think that this soldier had "...changed from something to nothing in less than a second."

Fisher had moved on then, keeping to his business. That was all he had left—doing what he was trained to do. Next, he had come across a body straddling a log. It was evident to Fisher the soldier had been trying to get over the deadfall when he had been riddled with bullets. Fisher had business to attend to, and people to help; he moved quickly over the log himself.

On the other side of the log sat a shot-up NCO. This sergeant had a sucking chest wound; blood and breath were gurgling together from the wound. Fisher knew that the man would drown in his own blood unless he acted quickly. He bandaged the wound and then taped the plastic wrapper from the bandage over both the dressing and wound "...in an effort to make it as airtight as possible." After several tense moments, the trooper began to breathe easier. When he could talk, he informed Fisher about the soldier stranded outside the perimeter. His buddy was thirty yards beyond the Americans' lines, out where that CS gas was thicker; out where the gas painted the battlefield with a milky pallor.

Fisher expected to die. But until that particular bullet hit him, or that piece of shrapnel stopped him; he decided to keep to his job of helping the wounded. He crawled on his belly toward the stricken man. Artillery, American artillery, was falling outside the perimeter. Fisher kept on moving despite the shell bursts. Close by; two artillery rounds went off simultaneously. He felt a sting; that was all. He thought he had snagged his uniform on a branch. "When I reached back I felt...blood and the shrapnel...sticking out of my shoulder." The fragment was small, so Fisher had no trouble picking it out of his shoulder and putting it in his pocket. Confirmation that he was going to die, all the men of the company were going to die.

Yet Fisher kept about his business. He left the wounded soldier near Robinson while he crawled back to the command post (approximately in the center of the 1st and 2nd platoons' locations). There Sergeant John D. Fulford was waiting to die. Fulford was just waiting, sitting on the ground and talking to himself. Talking rather calmly about how he would never see again, how he was blind. Sergeant Fulford had been shot in the head.

Fisher relates what happened next:

"I came up on a man who had been shot in the face. His left eye was gone and there was blood flowing from his broken jaw. Somehow, his glasses remained on his face. I didn't know whether the damage had been caused by one or more projectiles. I patched his eye right away but had some trouble with his jaw. I gave him a bandage to bite down on as he had lost most of his teeth on the left side. Finally, I managed to cover his jaw with a bandage and stop the bleeding..."[123]

Bullets were thick in the air, so Fisher had crawled up behind the sitting Fulford and said, "I can't get to your head but if you just drop back you'll land in my lap." Fulford did so. Fisher did not want to remove the man's helmet because it provided a modicum of protection, yet trying to affix the bandage over the shattered eye and adhere the bandage to the helmet was a major trial for the medic. Not the scattered brains of the ammunition-ladened soldier blasted through the head. Not the sucking chest wound of the NCO behind the log. Not even the shouts of pain or the overwhelming intensity of the firefight all around him now gripped him, only the problem with getting that bandage to stick to Fulford's helmet. The war, the frustration, the fear, and the sadness became focused on Sergeant John D. Fulford's helmet.

Fulford had been hit by a sniper hidden in a tree. The sergeant had taken a position at a machine gun after the 2nd Platoon's breakout attempt failed. Immediately after Fulford settled in, the assistant gunner sprang up to run and was stitched up the back with three sniper rounds. Then the sniper got Fulford. The bullet had plunged from above. Luckily for Fulford, the bullet had clipped the rim of his steel pot, deflecting the projectile just enough that though it pulverized his eye, it did not punch through his skull. He had thought that he was dead – no one survives a head wound. After a moment, he removed his helmet and felt around the back of his head. There was no exit wound. Fulford began to think he would make it. Someone had come along and helped him further back into the perimeter, where Lieutenants Libs and Fox were calling in the artillery strikes. After Fisher patched him up,[§] Fulford sat there in the CP area for the remainder of the battle, clutching two grenades in his hands in case the Vietcong broke through. Fulford did not intend on being taken alive.

Fulford was not as safe in this rear area as he might have liked. The perimeter had been whittled down to such a size that no place was safe – the enemy's .51 caliber machine gun shells were slicing through the entire area occupied by Company C. Also, snipers, such as those who had wounded Fulford and Captain Nolen, still infested the trees within the perimeter.

At one point, two radiomen from 1st Platoon, Roger Harris (Sergeant Sutterfield's RTO) and Bobby Holton (Lieutenant DeVoe's RTO), who were in the interior of the perimeter, found themselves bracketed by AK47 rounds. Harris and Holton were two of the youngest members of Charlie Company – Harris had been pulled out of the field in November 1965 because he was only seventeen – and both were radiomen because Platoon Sergeant Sutterfield was looking out for the youngsters. Radio operators were usually found in the middle of columns and certainly never walked point and so had an added measure of safety not available for other GIs. Not that that measure of protection was helping the two soldiers at that particular moment.

Bobby Holton, already wounded by shrapnel, leaned against a tree and watched as an unseen gunman was blasting off the bark from his refuge. He was watching the bullets rip into the trees when he finally spotted the sniper's vantage point—leaves were shaking high up in a tree about twenty yards in front of him. Holton figured that the leaves were shielding the sniper that was zeroing in on him. However, Holton could do little to stop the enemy sharpshooter because the RTO carried only a .45 caliber pistol, and he knew the pistol did not have the range to shoot up into that tree. "I could see that every time the son-of-a-bitch fired, the leaves would move, so I told Roger Harris."

Roger Harris had already hit bottom. Fear had gripped him after 1st Platoon's assault to break out had faltered. "I held onto my helmet and tried to get my whole body inside of it. A VC could have walked up to me and put a bullet in me." The fear shamed the young Virginian, and he told himself he did not want to die so pathetically. He reached inside himself and pulled up a prayer. He asked God to help him overcome his fear so that he might fight and live.

"The shooting and screaming continued but suddenly it seemed quiet to me. My fear was gone and I was able to move." The prayers had tamped down the overpowering fear. Harris became a functioning, fighting Charlie Company component.[124]

He found himself next to the 1st Platoon's commander, Lieutenant Smith DeVoe. DeVoe began using Harris' radio, while Harris readied his M16 for action. Harris had to keep shimmying around the tree to keep the radio available for DeVoe as the lieutenant scooted along the base of the trunk to avoid the bullets gnawing at the tree. Then Holton caught Harris' attention. Holton was pointing into the trees. Harris watched for a moment, caught the muzzle flash from the leaves. Harris said a prayer and raised his rifle. He pulled the trigger. Then Harris dropped the barrel just a tad and fired a second round.

"Harris dropped him…[the sniper] with his second shot," related a grateful Bob Holton years later.

"Did you get him?" asked Lieutenant DeVoe as he turned to look at Harris.

The body dropped from the tree at that point. DeVoe shouted, "We got one, we got one." With a yell, Holton promised Harris a case of beer, even though one soldier was too young to purchase the case while Harris was too young to drink it.[125]

Harris was not the only one attempting to knock the snipers from the trees. Sergeant Charles Weyant, heading up the communications section, searched for shooters in the trees above the CP area. He shot three and four-round bursts into likely airy locales, but he just never saw the enemy. It was a shame too. Weyant had been on several marksman teams while serving in the military, but no proper shot presented itself.

For James Finney, the problem was the same as Weyant's: he was threatened by sniper fire from the trees, but he could not see the enemy up there. Finney was new to Vietnam—one week new to the unit. He had the further misfortune of being in 3rd Platoon, which meant by this time in the battle – as the CS gas was seeping into his eyes, as machine guns were burning the air above his head, as the cries of the American wounded grew into relentless shouts in his ears, Finney found himself retreating in a crawl away from that big log and the corpses of many 3rd Platoon comrades. It was all terrifyingly strange to Finney, and the retreat was no better because the ground next to him was being aerated with sniper shots coming from the same direction he was retreating into!

Finney aimed at a muzzle flash high in the foliage and squeezed off a burst. A soldier beside him did the same. Then Finney was paralyzed, a bullet crashing into his right shoulder, the shell exploding on impact with the collar bone and pulverizing the bones and muscle nearby. Finney passed out momentarily. By the time he awoke, there were no Americans around him and no light except the haunting illumination rounds sinking slowly earthward from the helicopters flying overhead continuously through the night. He stayed where he had been hit for the remainder of the night. Any movement sent paroxysms of pain jolting through his body as shards of shattered bones ground together. Finney's tour of Vietnam would be over when he was medevacked with the dawn.

Sergeant Robinson of 1st Platoon was on course for his fateful encounter with the snipers, but before those killers in the trees attracted his attention Robinson was determined to kill as many Vietcong on the ground as he could. Historian Andrew Woods explained what happened next as Robinson, focused "on his own wounds…" patching "them with hasty dressings and" giving himself "a shot of morphine."[126]

Robinson refused to crawl, instead maintaining a crouching position as he charged about the perimeter. "Sergeant Robinson…was…the most adrenalin-charged man I ever saw," related Sergeant Weyant, who observed Robinson during one of the former Marine's brief respites in the CP area. Weyant viewed Robinson as "totally committed to killing as many VC as possible." When he was not occupied in gunning down the enemy, he gathered up the weapons of the dead and wounded and redistributed them to the able.

Robinson seized an M79 grenade launcher when he realized snipers were firing from the trees. The sergeant bolted from the command post, darted through the perimeter until he spotted the shooter, then lobbed a shell up into the trees where it blew the sniper to pieces. By this time, other snipers and machine gunners had zeroed in on the rampaging sergeant, their tracers streaking through the gathering gloom to hit him in the leg. Robinson moved back to the CP with one pant leg of his uniform on fire from the tracers. He pulled out his K-bar knife and cut away the smoldering cloth. Weyant expected Robinson to join the other wounded in the CP (besides the leg wound, Robinson had taken a bullet in the shoulder). Instead, Robinson cursed the enemy—who were still targeting him specifically—and charged again toward the perimeter.

The dead and wounded were everywhere. Robinson had run out of ammunition for his M16. The situation was desperate. It was a time and place tailor-made for a hero. Instead of calculating, going to ground, Robinson saw the muzzle flash from the .51 caliber machine gun and shouted out, "I see the .50. I'm going for it. Cover me." Author George Wilson describes Robinson's next moves.

> "Robinson pulled two grenades off his web belt. He yanked out the pins so they were ready to go off once he let his fingers off the spoon firing mechanism running down the side of the grenade…With a Marine growl, Robinson ran toward the .50, one grenade in each hand."[127]

Wilson states that the tracer round that torched Robinson's pant leg hit then – rather than earlier as Weyant remembers.[§§] Wilson continues, writing that Robinson "staggered to within 10 yards of the machine gun despite its withering fire," took both grenades in his one good hand, and hurled them "smack into the machine-gun position." The grenades went off just as a staccato burst from the .51 blasted Robinson in the chest, killing him instantly.[128]

That is more or less the official story of Robinson's deeds and death. There is also another version of Robinson's death—an eyewitness version. This second story coincides with the Army's version in most respects except for how Robinson met his death.

In the eyewitness version, Robinson made it back to the perimeter after knocking out the machine gun. If that is correct, he would not have been hit by the .51 because .51 caliber slugs make subway-sized holes in a man. Wounded that grievously the sergeant would have almost certainly been unable to return to the perimeter. Yet there he was, still adrenaline-pumped, still maddened by the snipers who were pouring down death from their perches high in the trees. Again, Robinson grabbed up a grenade launcher and began shouting, "they're in the trees, they're in the trees," as he blooped grenades into the branches above him.

Pfc Milton Lader had been crawling toward the CP—the men were pulling back from the perimeter—when he witnessed Robinson making this run through the trees. Robinson was a madman, oblivious to the danger he was in by running upright. Lader rolled onto his back and sprayed the trees with rifle fire. He glanced over toward Robinson and saw the big man driven to the ground from a sniper round. Robinson was dead.‡‡

It is possible that what Lader saw was Robinson being hit for the first time in the shoulder. It is possible that Robinson stood after receiving the wound that Lader witnessed, and that the sergeant continued in his actions until that .51 caliber machine gun took him down. This is one of those facts that the fog of war will forever obscure. It should be noted, however, that of the more than fifty men interviewed or otherwise contacted for their recollections of the battle, none offered that they had seen Robinson go down – except Milton Lader. Furthermore, when explicitly asked for someone to step forward and say they saw Robinson killed by machine-gun fire, none of the men contacted did so.†

Whether Robinson died in a blaze of glory as he eliminated the machine gun raking 1st Platoon's area, or whether it was a bullet from a sniper that killed him, the sergeant who had set his sights on a Medal of Honor, deserved the award that was bestowed on him posthumously. He had "assisted in eliminating a major enemy threat" when he, Heath, Walden, and Steele halted the Vietcong charge that could have resulted in the company being cut in two. Robinson had "charged through a withering hail of fire and dragged his comrades to safety," rescuing a wounded man and the 2nd Platoon medic, Bob Fisher, when Fisher had called for help. He pinpointed the location of snipers in the trees and "took a grenade launcher and eliminated the sniper[s]." And he charged a machine gun that "had inflicted a number of casualties on the American force," and blew it up despite the intense fire that was directed toward him. And finally, Robinson did sacrifice his life to save the lives of his comrades; whether that sacrifice occurred from a machine gun burst or a sniper's bullet is irrelevant to his heroism. The alternate story is set out here to give voice to the concerns of so many of the Charlie Company veterans who doubt the veracity of the official account of Robinson's death.

..

Burt Heath was another soldier felled by snipers. He had rushed out with Sergeant Robinson to stop the assaulting VC and then he had gone out again when Bradley attempted to knock out the .51 caliber machine gun. Returning from his second sortie outside the perimeter, Heath caught both shrapnel and a sniper round in the back. The bullet passed through his body and exited through his chest.[∞] He was temporarily knocked cold, but miraculously the wound was clean, missing vital organs—Heath would be among the walking wounded the following day. However, for the moment, like fellow 1st Platoon members, Inkelaar and Bradley, Heath was out.

Snipers had already taken their toll on the 4th Platoon. As the guerrillas made their third attempt to roll over the 4th Platoon's area, the snipers had stepped up their firing into the remnants of Lieutenant Steinberg's men. The GIs of the 4th Platoon were not quiescent during this renewed assault. Several soldiers hurled CS canisters and smoke grenades at the onrushing enemy. Other Americans continued to pour M16 fire into the trees. As noted earlier, the wind blew the tear gas and smoke back into the American lines, but this helped obscure the platoon's positions, protecting them from the snipers above.

In the case of Sergeant Harold Hunter, the smoke probably saved his life. Staff Sergeant Bozy Gerald—Hunter's friend besides being his superior—had taken the full burst from a grenade. Gerald was lying out in the open, calling for help. Hunter jumped to grab Gerald and drag him to a safer position when a sniper bullet slammed into Hunter's thigh—a shot likely meant for the heart or head that went south due to the smoke.

Unfortunately for Hunter, he fell directly behind a Claymore mine set up by another 4th Platoon trooper. As the Vietcong approached, the other American set off the Claymore. The blast vaporized several of the guerillas, while the concussion knocked Hunter unconscious. Hunter would not awaken until complete darkness had descended on the battlefield, and the scene to which he would awaken was so horrifying it was as if he were still unconscious and trapped in a nightmare.

This assault marked the high-water mark for the guerillas, not that anyone in Company C realized that. From the point of the 4th Platoon's repulse of the third assault until the battle sputtered away in the darkness, the VC continued to pour in a deadly fire while maneuvering to overrun the Americans; however, the enemy would never actually launch another concerted attack. The artillery shield that the XO Ken Alderson and 2nd Platoon's John Libs were calling down to ring the perimeter would be tight enough and sustained enough to deter any other assault attempts by the Vietcong. Besides, Vietcong tactics typically called for a brutal strike near dusk and then a quick retreat into the jungle under cover of darkness.

Sergeant Schoolman of the 3rd Platoon certainly did not feel any slackening of pressure from the enemy. The sergeant had managed to pull portions of his squad farther away from the machine guns' grazing fire—considering the intensity of the fire that was an accomplishment—but he and his men were isolated. Schoolman could not see any other Americans. He decided to find out who, if anyone, was on his right. Schoolman looked at his men and, gesturing to his right, said, "Don't shoot in that direction. I'll be out there."

He crawled away from the slight cover where he had been concealed, and too quickly bullets began cracking over his head. A couple of rounds dinged off his helmet. Schoolman tried to increase his speed even as he dug a furrow in the ground from crawling so low. His web gear became entangled in some brush. The sergeant could not move forward. He could not move back. Small fountains of earth spouted all around him. He had to do something or he would be planted permanently on that piece of real estate.

Schoolman unbuckled his gas mask and web gear and slithered out of the paraphernalia. He scrambled several feet, found some shelter, and looked up to see the CS gas cloud come drifting his way. The sergeant gagged, cried, and continued his move to the right. Beyond the bush or termite mound or clot of dirt where he had temporarily found safety was a free-fire zone. The bullets were zinging by, the gas was choking him, and the American artillery was pounding down. Schoolman was shot in the lower leg between the knee and ankle.

He found a standing tree and leaned his back against it. He looked back the way he had just come, the cloud of gas, the tracers piercing the area and the ground exploding, and he thought, "Schoolman, that was stupid." He took out his medic bag as the bullets tugged at his shirt sleeves and kicked up the dirt at the base of the tree, ripped open the pants leg, and applied the bandage to the wound. He glanced at the other side of his leg and saw blood streaming from the exit wound. He tore a sleeve off his fatigues and tied that around the exit wound.

"Garner, I'm hit, take the squad," he yelled back toward his men.

Schoolman still could see no one to his right, and he had long since lost sight of his men to his left. He had to do something, move somewhere because that tree was attracting a lot of lead. The NCO began crawling toward the right once more, but this time to better his situation rather than find any 3rd Platoon troopers.

If Schoolman could have been lifted at that moment — just as darkness was about to extinguish the remaining light – and float above that battlefield and thus survey it, he would have been dismayed at the scene beneath him. No healthy 3rd Platoon GIs remained in the direction Schoolman was heading. Sergeant Navarro's squad had been holding down that sector of the 3rd Platoon's area, but Navarro had been wounded early on and carried deep into the perimeter. The assault by Langston out of the perimeter and the resulting enemy counterpunch had shattered the squad's remaining manpower. There on the 3rd Platoon's right flank, clustered around an ant mound or jammed behind a tree trunk, were the wounded and frightened, but there was no line. Behind Schoolman, where he had left his squad on the platoon's left, he might catch a glimpse of Burris, and Lang (who had found his way back to the squad) shielded behind a skinny tree. He could have seen Spec 4 Richard Garner forced away from that big log that lay closer to the Vietcong base camp. The NCO would have seen no less than three corpses behind that log, one of those being the body of Sergeant Seasholtz. Beyond the log, out farther to the left, just where the artillery was screeching down through the blasted trees and churning up the earth, he would have seen a heap of bodies. If the confusion of battle had not disoriented him too completely, he might have remembered that this was the location where Lieutenant Kroah had been wounded.

The scene sliding off to Kroah's left would have crushed whatever hope Schoolman retained, for there amongst the CS cloud, the shell craters, and the blasted terrain lay the bodies of 4th Platoon. There were no healthy men in that direction; the survivors had retreated. All that remained were the dead and the seriously wounded.

But Schoolman was not some Icarus flying in the treetops. The ring of death hemming in the unit was not visible in its totality. Instead, as night fell, the sergeant was blindly crawling on, not knowing the situation, not knowing the extent of the harm done, not knowing even where he was scrambling. Flares began to illuminate the jungle with their spiraling, ghost-like descent. Schoolman came across a trooper propped up against a tree. The soldier was crying.

"Where are you hurt?"

"My stomach."

In the crazy ghost-light of the flares, Schoolman could see that the front of the soldier's uniform was black from blood. Schoolman scooted up next to the GI and reached over and took his hand. "I held his hand all night."

---

*John's sister provided me with a letter to John's parents that had been written by Captain Nolen sometime after the battle. Using Nolen's description of John's actions as my guide I have placed John in 2nd Platoon's area during the battle.

±In 4th platoon's area, men had thrown CS canisters (tear gas) and smoke grenades to stifle a third assault attempt. The wind blew the noxious fumes back over Charlie Company's position. For several minutes the Americans had to contend with the gas as well as the Vietcong.

**Fisher went where the cries of help led him; he was not even in the 2nd platoon's sector any longer.

§The bullet destroyed Fulford's right eye, not his left, as Fisher remembered.

§§The citation for the Medal of Honor also states that Robinson's clothes were ignited at this time.

‡‡Another veteran told me this story months before I met Mr. Lader. However, that veteran was merely passing on the eyewitness account from another soldier, Burt Heath. The morning after the battle, as the survivors gathered up the dead, Heath reported having seen Robinson killed by a sniper the night before. Sadly, Burt Heath died of a heart attack some years before research on this book began. Until Milton Lader entered that hotel conference room in Nashville during the first Charlie Company Reunion in the summer of 2001 and spoke, I had resigned myself to leaving the story alone. However, Mr. Lader, in that friendly, never-met-a-stranger way of his, launched into—as he entered that conference room—a five-minute unprompted reminiscence about the battle that ended with his account of Robinson's death. I had my eyewitness.

† On January 22, 2005, I sent an e-mail out to 37 Company veterans. No one responded with an affirmation of the official story. Marty Kroah simply commented that "Robinson didn't die the way his citation said." Throughout working on this project, other company veterans have voiced their disbelief in the official story.

[∞] It is possible that before Heath fell from his wounds, he also witnessed Sergeant Robinson's death. See the footnote referring to Robinson's death.

Chapter Six:
The Longest Night

"Someone stepped on me…I had passed out after being shot…When I got stepped on I woke up, but something in that split second before opening my eyes told me to keep'em closed, not to react."

Harold Hunter

"I'm going to die a virgin."

Burt Heath

The wounded and the dead outnumbered the healthy. Many of the wounded had been carried back to the command post. At the CP, medics like Dave Marchetti and Bob Fisher did what they could to "doctor" the wounded, but the medics were running low on morphine and bandages. Airman Pitsenbarger continued his efforts to comfort the wounded who sprawled on the ground. Pitsenbarger was the Pararescue team member who volunteered to be lowered from the helicopter's relative safety to the battlefield below. Then he waved off the return ride up in the litter. However, Pitsenbarger was not satisfied to let the wounded be brought to him.

Amid the swarm of lead hurtling through the air, Pitsenbarger "crawled through the...jungle looking for wounded soldiers." Finding them—for there were plenty to be found—the airman would "drag them to the middle of the...perimeter, putting them behind trees and logs for shelter." Many of the wounded were outside the perimeter, in no-man's land. One GI recalled Pitsenbarger spotting two shot-up troopers lying beyond the perimeter. "We've got to go get those people!" Pitsenbarger said. The GI responded, "No way. I'm staying behind my tree." Pitsenbarger darted out into "unbelievable fire" to get to the two wounded men. At the sight of the fearless airman risking his life for strangers, the reluctant GI was inspired to follow, and together the two of them retrieved the two wounded men.[129]

Later, Pitsenbarger picked up a rifle and fought alongside the men of Company C. He also was careful to protect one gravely wounded soldier, Sergeant Fred Navarro of the 3rd Platoon. Navarro was looking particularly bad, he had lost a prodigious amount of blood, and Pitsenbarger knew the sergeant was too weak to defend himself. The airman went to Navarro and pulled two American corpses over the sergeant to protect him from incoming fire. The airman also went through the perimeter, gathering up rifles and ammunition. He redistributed these valuable items where the defenders needed them the most. A newbie, in Vietnam only eleven days, recalled Pitsenbarger appearing with ammunition when the soldier was running low.

"Imagine four or five hundred guns firing at the same time. I knew I was about out of ammunition. I had my face down in the dirt, I was afraid to move more than anything else. I realized someone was coming across this little opening and just dropped three magazines on me and I think he asked 'are you OK?' Then he was gone."[130]

Finally, Pitsenbarger's amazing run ended. Navarro watched as the brave man headed out toward another wounded soldier only to be struck several times by enemy fire.[131*]

Dan Kirby was among the 3rd Platoon's wounded. As the 3rd Squad of 3rd Platoon shattered under the enemy's hammer blows, Kirby—before he was wounded—found himself falling back to a position behind a standing tree where four or five other men had taken refuge. Kirby assumed a prone position to return fire in the direction from which he had come only to have a bullet smash into his lower leg, ripping along his calf. A flesh wound.

"To my left behind the tree was a dead [man], slumped over a still smoking M60 machine gun. To my right was an older sergeant, sitting with his back straight up the tree and what was left of his legs at a 90-degree angle from his torso. His legs were obviously mangled and broken [from] the [unnatural] angle of his feet. He was praying out loud and I asked him to 'pray for me too' which he did."

Small arms fire was splatting against the front of the tree, spraying splinters left and right. A grenade "thumped" against the tree and fell out of reach but within lethal range. Kirby thought, "that was the end," but the grenade fizzled like some sinister firecracker and died without exploding.

> "Soon another soldier whom I believed to be a medic, joined us behind the tree and he began working on the sergeant's leg wounds. While doing so he [the medic] took two rounds, very quickly together, in his face. He looked straight at me, it seemed like a long time, but probably only a couple of seconds and then fell face down on the [sergeant's] legs."

The sergeant died, and the wounded Kirby caught sight of some "shadowy figures" skulking toward his location. It was time for the soldier to move again. Luckily, it was dark by this time, so Kirby was able to hobble into the new perimeter.

In 2nd Platoon's area, James "Rick" Owens was isolated behind a five-foot-tall concrete-solid anthill and the young Kentuckian was taking fire. "My helmet flew off my head and I felt a sting in my neck (shrapnel had chipped his fourth vertebra). I thought I was dead." Owens reached around and put his hand on the wound and the sensation of feeling the blood pumping out of the ripped flesh convinced the rifleman that he was dying.

Out there alone, Owens administered himself first aid, applying a bandage the best that he could and gaining his composure as the bleeding seemed to slow. He was just beginning to feel better about his situation when he was shot in his left shoulder.

Besides the wounded, Charlie Company's men had to fight the Vietcong with another impediment weighing them down;

some of the men were too frightened to fight. Pfc Galen Summerlot, the "fresh meat" GI who had complained in a letter to his parents that he might never see action, had scrambled backward when the 2nd Platoon's assault had failed. He came across another soldier who convinced Summerlot that if Summerlot could find an entrenching tool, he [the other soldier] would dig a hole big enough for the both of them. Summerlot thought that was a swell idea, crawled back toward the incoming fire far enough to find a discarded entrenching tool, and with the prized shovel in his hands, returned to the frightened soldier. The soldier snatched away the shovel, quickly scooped out a hole snug enough for one, and ignored the exposed Summerlot.

1st Platoon's Sergeant Faberski was crawling about gathering weapons when he noticed that many of the men were not firing their rifles. They seemed frozen, unable to act. When he came across one cowering sergeant from another platoon, Faberski thought to bully the man back into action by shouting at him, "Get to your men." The non-com ignored Faberski. Faberski moved toward the man, a big man known for his quick smile and happy nature. On April 11, however, he was not a good-natured sort, for as Faberski approached him, the man growled, "Stay away or I'll kill your fuckin' ass!" Faberski believed him, turning away to collect more weapons.

Another soldier broken by the battle was the sergeant who had gone berserk when the first errant rounds of artillery had slammed into the company area. The same sergeant that Pfc Doug Blankenheim had jumped on and slapped to snap him back to his senses. As the battle continued, this sergeant did not fight. He did not move. Gripping his rifle and ammunition, the sergeant simply lay down and refused to budge. He did not fire his weapon, but neither would he give up the rifle or the ammunition when others ran short of ammunition or needed a new weapon.[132]

Lieutenant Kroah, years later, commented that some of the men, "...just laid down—never fought, never fired their weapons." These were replacements who had worried Sergeants Sutterfield and Langston earlier in the day. Over sixty new men in the company in the last month. Not their fault that they had walked into the most one-sided battle America encountered in its first year in Vietnam. The number who failed to defend themselves is unclear. The number was never large, not among the new men or the old hands.

Yet some old hands did fold, like the sergeant encountered by Faberski or the manic sergeant confronted by Blankenheim. Moreover, there were men on the perimeter who might have glanced back at the CP area and saw healthy officers and enlisted men huddled there and thought they were witnessing cowardice. In those instances, with death staring them in the face, soldiers had only the belief—as expressed by Bob Fisher—that each soldier could count on every other soldier to do his duty. "It could only work, we could only survive, if we all did our part." Fisher then explains that "it's easy to see that anyone with these feelings would be angered to believe that some of these men were not doing their part." Fisher faced something like this need to know everyone was contributing to the defense, but rather than project cowardice onto others, he swallowed his fear and redoubled his efforts. He vowed that he would do his part by attending to the wounded ever more efficiently. Despite his resolution, the medic believes that he knows how those frontline soldiers felt as they caught sight of someone shirking—or someone whom they thought was shirking – at the CP. "I can imagine some of the [men] feeling like, 'I suffer all of this fear, all of the horror and risk my life, and you—you, whoever you might be, are a coward.' I suppose that I was fortunate not to witness any acts of real cowardice. What I saw was a group of brave men fight for each other." Roger Harris, the 1st Platoon radio operator who found himself near the command post area along with Lieutenant Smith DeVoe and the other officers, adds another possible explanation for what some GIs saw as cowardice, "Those of us in the center could not shoot anywhere but up since we would likely hit our own men. Also, we couldn't see the enemy." Harris was the kid, the youngest member of the company, and also the man who took out a sniper after his fellow radioman, Bobby Holton, had pointed to the enemy in the trees. Harris received the Bronze Star for his actions at Xa Cam My and has never received anything but the highest praise from Charlie Company veterans who knew him. He goes on to explain the situation in the center of the perimeter:

> "Any of us could have been accused of being a coward during some point in the battle. When the battle was at its highest pitch no one could move without getting hit and many got hit even when they weren't moving. I'm not the only survivor who was frozen with fear for several minutes. Many of us cowards were able to overcome that fear and were later considered to be heroes. Many survivors are ashamed that they were frozen with fear, but I think most of them made some contribution to our survival and should not be ashamed."

Again, from Harris: "Any of us could have been accused of being a coward during some point of the battle." Fisher said, "What I saw was a group of brave men fight for each other." Lieutenant Libs certainly was among the men that both Fisher's and Harris' words could have characterized. Libs himself recalls, "There were many times I hugged the ground to keep from getting hit...I remember on one occasion [digging] a little hole to put my head in so the CS gas wouldn't get to me and make me throw up. I didn't have a gas mask... If anybody saw that, I'm sure they thought I was trying to dig my way out of the battle." Libs has also made an observation similar to Bob Fisher's comments about appearances in the area of the command post, "I'm sure there could be many more 'snap shots' during the battle that would seem like indifference on my part...I was in the 'get-it-done' mode! I was so busy on the radio, as well as preparing for what I believed would be a full-scale assault on the platoon."

The other officers at the command post were also working feverishly on the radios, trying to save the company. Sergeant Charles Weyant of the communication section remembers Lieutenant Alderson in contact with the many hovering helicopters over the battlefield, giving situation reports to headquarters. Sergeant Faberski, scrounging for weapons, came across Lieutenant Fox. Faberski could see the artillery forward observer was diligently sending out the coordinates for the artillery, and in a matter-of-fact tone, telling whoever was on the other end of the radio, "You better get us out of here or there won't be anything left to get out!" Lieutenant DeVoe conferred with Fox and Libs about bringing the artillery directly in on the Americans' location when things looked darkest. Roger Harris felt that each officer did what they could, writing, "When a company is in a defensive perimeter the officers are not supposed to be on the perimeter. They are supposed to be behind the lines of their men, and their radio operators are supposed to be with them."

In the tropics, sunset comes in a rush. By the time the weary Americans had fought off the third assault, it was dark. Then the enemy commander had to assess the situation and decide whether to strike again or to make good his getaway over the network of jungle trails that had, since the beginning of Operation ABILENE, allowed the battalion avenues of escape when combat with the Americans had not been to his advantage. The commander would have received reports of the other American units' movements and weighed that information in his decision.$^{\pm}$ As darkness engulfed the battlefield, perhaps D800's leader postponed a definitive decision to see how events developed further, or maybe he wanted to inflict more damage on the crippled Americans. The VC continued to let their presence be known but did not press a new attack.

With darkness closing in on the men, a new and terrifying horror crept onto the battlefield. The incoming fire diminished. Some thought it ceased altogether, others that it only slackened. Even as the sound of firing diminished, it was replaced by a woeful sound, a maddening sound that ripped at the psyche of those soldiers within the perimeter. It was the anguished calls of the wounded beyond the perimeter.

"I've never heard such screaming in my life," Pfc Ronald Haley, the impromptu machine gunner from 1st Platoon, would tell a news reporter flown to the battle site the next day. "Many of the wounded were yelling for their mothers. Some of the kids were calling for God."

They called for their deity or their mother; some called for their friends in the company. Randall "Peanuts" Prinz lay somewhere in the no-man's-land in front of 3rd Platoon and called out for his close friend Richard Garner. The thought of the kid hurt and beyond reach was maddening. "Garner, I'm hit." Lang would shout out, "hold on Peanuts, I'm coming," though the bullets and the wounds kept him from moving. Garner and Burris were behind the same tree where Lang had sought shelter, but both had been wounded by nightfall and were unable to help their friend. With darkness, the trio was startled to hear another voice, much closer, ask for help. Burris managed to look beyond the tree trunk's shelter to see a wounded Pfc David A. Hammett crawling up the slope. "He'd almost bled out. I've never seen anyone so white," Dave Burris described Hammett's appearance. "His right arm is nothing but meat." The firing was too heavy for the men behind the tree to move.

The tracers were thick and ominous looking in the gathering darkness. "It looks like the VC are shooting red hot beer cans at us. [Hammett] reaches the base of a tree to our right and he leans against it." Hammett says, "My arm." Burris and Garner were yelling for Hammett to take his belt off and make a tourniquet to stop the bleeding. No one moved. The firing was like a blade six inches off the ground, slicing, slicing. Hammett managed to get his belt off, but he could not wrap it around the stump of his arm. He was too weak. Still, Garner and Burris shouted encouragement until a bullet slammed into Hammett's chest. "He flopped over."

Unknown to his friends in the 3rd Platoon, Randall "Peanuts" Prinz was crawling around in no-man's-land seeking help. He ended up in front of Pfc Leroy Love. Love spotted the wounded Prinz just as Prinz spotted him. Prinz called out for Love to help him. Love told the kid known as "Peanuts" to stay down. Love can only conjecture that Peanuts was delirious with pain because, despite Love's warning, Peanuts continued to crawl toward him. With Love looking on helplessly, the .51 caliber machine gun swung its deadly aim at Peanuts. A slug found Prinz, tearing through a shoulder. The bullet's force killed him instantly.

One person most survivors from the company recall hearing that night was Sergeant Bozy Gerald. Gerald, severely wounded by grenade fragments, had managed to prop himself up against a tree in what once had been the 4th Platoon's area. Gerald and the unconscious Sergeant Harold Hunter were outside the perimeter, and Gerald was calling for help. There was anguish, pain, and fury rolled up and bellowed out in bursts of cursing and plaintive cries for help. Gerald screeched at the men of Charlie Company to help him. Then Gerald roared at the Americans to kill him.

Sergeant Faberski hunkered down near the wounded Platoon Sergeant Sutterfield and endured Gerald's screams until he could no longer stand it. Faberski started for the perimeter only to be called back by Sutterfield. "You won't make it," Sutterfield told him simply. Faberski stopped his crawling and continued to listen to Gerald's and the other wounded men's cries.

Now full dark, with the eerie light from the flares the only illumination, the company was in for another jolt. From first one side of the perimeter, then the other came the magnified voices of men shouting through megaphones. Libs looked at the Vietnamese interpreter and asked, "what are they saying?"

The interpreter responded, "They are getting ready for the final attack."[133]

Lieutenants Libs, Alderson, DeVoe, and the forward artillery observer, Lieutenant Fox, discussed bringing the artillery barrage directly down on the company. Libs instructed Underwood to bring the artillery virtually on top of Charlie Company. The barrage came down, but too far out, too far out for Libs' liking. "Bring it closer! It's our only chance!"

Mud Soldiers author George Wilson describes the scene: "It sounded…as if freight trains were coming down… from the sky. The artillery shells hurtling in whizzed, hissed, and whooshed before plunging into the ground."[134] The artillery battery supporting Company C was sending in a screaming munitions shield for the Americans. The ring closed down any further attack by the enemy. Phil Hall of 2nd Platoon was convinced it was Libs' bold orders over the radio that saved the platoon from a final mass attack. The time was 5:57 PM.[135]

All around the shrunken perimeter, men understood the implications of the VC's shouts, if not the exact words. 3rd Platoon's Dan Kirby, who had found his way to a spot next to Steve Antal of 2nd Platoon—who supplied a t-shirt that Kirby used as a bandage for his wounded leg—heard Libs discussing the expected charge with the Vietnamese interpreter. Kirby thought it was over. "I'm dead," he told himself. The realization that there was no escape calmed Kirby. He decided that he would fire off all his clips before he died. And so, he calmly waited for the onslaught.

Sergeant Sutterfield looked at his close friend Sergeant Pete Faberski and said, "Well Pete, I think that's it. How many clips do you have?" Faberski gave Sutterfield an estimate of his remaining ammunition. Sutterfield then said, "Organize the troops. Have our men face toward 3rd and 4th platoons' positions. That's where they will be coming from."

Milton Lader took a Claymore mine and quickly lifted himself, bent over the log behind which he had sheltered, planted the mine, and then plunked himself back down behind the log. "We didn't aim it [the mine] at nothin'. Just figured we'd take some with us before we died."

The radioman Gilbert Delao found himself next to a machine gunner from another platoon.** The machine gunner was carrying an M16, but Delao knew him as part of a machine gun crew. Both men got word that the Vietcong were coming. " Both the gunner and I rounded up any weapons we could find to repel them. Even got out entrenching tools."

Sergeant Weyant understood the situation. The Americans were low on ammunition, with an assault imminent. He thought the unit might be wiped out. "I laid out my grenades, flares, and radio codes and planned…to pull the pin off a white phosphorus grenade to prevent the enemy from taking the lists of codes and frequencies," Weyant explained his methodical actions. "I…also unsheathed my machete."

Weyant had already faced death a few times—even before Vietnam, the sergeant had been stabbed in a knife fight and shot. He did not fear death, and as he thought about his family, a wife, and two sons, he took solace in the fact that his sons would carry on the family name. He had been in the Army eleven years, since he was sixteen, and the sergeant took considerable pride in his unit—they were the "Rangers" of the 16th Infantry Regiment—and there might be better places to die, but there were no better men with whom to die.

Bob Fisher had run out of medical supplies. He had made comfortable as many of the wounded as possible. He wanted to contribute somehow, but he knew he was not much of a shooting soldier. Loading M16s seemed like a useful alternative. He crawled over to Lieutenant Fox, the Forward Observer, and began ramming bullets into magazines. Fox took all the clips Fisher could load and stacked them to one side for later use. Fox and Fisher did not discover until morning that Fisher had been jamming the bullets in backward, making the clips useless. Thankfully no Americans asked to use those magazines that night. Fisher then received a direct order from Lieutenant Libs to take up a position on the line and "Shoot anything that moves." Libs repeated the instructions he had given after the failed breakout attempt, instructing Fisher to aim at the darkness and hang on. The lieutenant tapped Fisher on the back as he moved away.

Fisher's fear that he was going to be struck by an artillery shell subsided. His fear that the VC would sweep over the perimeter was growing.

"Earlier...on three or four occasions, the fighting would seem to have stopped....At each of those times, some part of me began to believe that it was over. Each time, I had been wrong. Now in the...darkness I wondered what the enemy was doing. I lay there, still, listened to the Artillery, and blindly watched a point of darkness. Maybe they [the enemy] were still out there, even somewhere between us and the explosions, preparing for the next...attack on our weakened force. For a long time I prayed that they were gone."[136]

Fisher's fear that the enemy had slipped in "...between us and the explosions..." was more than a scared young man's nightmare. It was standard tactics for the Vietcong. "Grab the belt"; moving in between the omnipresent American artillery shields and the Army unit/s under attack was a classic Vietnamese guerilla adaptation to the U.S. propensity to use their artillery to "pound enemy units" into oblivion.[137] In the case of the mangled Charlie Company, the idea was not to attack but to loot.

Pfc Ted Piner, who had been knocked unconscious in the 2nd Platoon's breakout attempt, awoke to find himself being dragged away by two Vietcong. The two guerillas, finding Piner's limp body, must have assumed that the Mississippian was dead because they were pulling him away from the perimeter by his web gear. Piner came fully awake but feinted death until the right moment arose. When he was first aware of what was happening to him, he also realized that his .45 was beneath him, next to the ground where he could not reach it. A moment or two passed, and the guerillas pulled the Pfc over a stump, which allowed him to snatch his pistol from his belt and drill one of the soldiers point-blank in the chest. The second guerilla slashed at Piner with a huge knife, opening up the

Particular Bravery: The Battle of Xa Cam My And The Death of a Grunt Company

Mississippian's right hand. Piner grabbed his knife and stabbed his enemy until the man died. Piner then gingerly picked his way back toward the perimeter.

Sergeant Manley's body had been dragged from the perimeter by the enemy. The tough sergeant, the steadying hand who had brought his squad through so much, was only discovered several hours after daylight on April 12. He was a hundred yards beyond any other American body.

Burt Heath, who had earlier taken a sniper round and shrapnel in his back, lay outside the perimeter feigning death. He could not move; his wounds and the mass of artillery prohibited attempting to reach the perimeter. Lying there among his dead comrades, his face in the dirt, Heath heard VC voices nearby. He lay still, playing opossum while the enemy moved through his area, picking at the bodies, removing equipment, and killing the wounded Americans they discovered. As a guerilla stepped over him, the frightened soldier had a thought flash through his brain, "I'm going to die a virgin." Fortunately for Heath, the Vietnamese looting the bodies bought his dead soldier act and did not touch him.

Out where so many of the 4th Platoon's men lay dead, Sergeant Harold Hunter was awakened when someone stepped on him. "Something in that split second before opening my eyes told me to keep'em closed." Intuition told him to play dead. "A second later whoever it was moved away from me. I opened my eyes just a fraction." What Hunter saw then has haunted him ever since that night. "I could make out a woman moving toward Bozy Gerald. He was sitting with his back against a tree. I saw the woman bend down to look in his face, and then shoot him in the head."

One group of wounded men whom Bob Fisher had assisted to a huge tree that seemed to be in a safe area were killed by the enemy. Other American wounded who cried out for help were approached and killed by Vietcong women. Dave Burris of 3rd Platoon was alone in the no-man's-land by this time, and he heard one American soldier call out, "Please don't." These marauders carried candles to find their way through the jungle. Some of them used knives to cut Americans' throats rather than use a bullet on the wounded.

Ho Chi Minh called the women soldiers of Vietnam the "Long-haired Warriors," and though it was more common for Vietnamese women to be found in support roles in Vietcong units—such as cooks and nurses—there were women who participated in combat.[138] The people of Vietnam had long revered women warriors for in their national history of resistance to foreigners two of their national heroes were the Trung Sisters who had successfully led a first century rebellion against the Chinese. In that same rebellion another female hero emerged when Phung Thi Chinh, demonstrated the people's tenacity when she gave birth on the battlefield then bundled the baby on to her back and continued fighting the country's enemies.[139] In the fight against Americans, women of local villages were expected to help build base camps and supply other logistical support. The women who ranged among the dead and wounded of Charlie Company could have been local women let loose on the Americans or local force guerillas who had been participating in the fight from its beginning. According to the official "Narrative—History of the Battle of Xa Cam My," the women "...also assisted the wounded VC as they began to cry for help. This operation was done in haste by these women as they pulled back for the last time." [140]

Pfc Harris had continued to work the radio when an American soldier radioed in from beyond the perimeter. It was Pfc Gregory L. Bishop from the 3rd Platoon. Bishop, known as "Bebop" to the company, was a conscientious objector who had served as Platoon Sergeant Langston's radioman. He was isolated out among the 3rd Platoon's dead and wounded. Bishop told Harris that Vietcong were moving around, robbing bodies. Harris emphasized to Bebop that the injured around him were counting on him to defend them. Bishop answered affirmatively, telling Harris that he had "picked up a .45 pistol," and the conscientious objector assured young Harris that he would use it if necessary.[141]‡

Lieutenant Kroah was already awake when he, his radioman Conway, and the 3rd Platoon medic heard the enemy approaching. The Vietnamese voices were high-pitched, women's voices. Kroah understood what was happening.

"Our only chance is to play dead when they get near us," Kroah said to the other men.[142]

> "The three of us held hands and said the Lord's Prayer. And played dead. They came over to our position. They rolled the radio operator over on top of me and took everything off his belt. They didn't touch me. They were men and women with them. And then they tried to take the first aid bag from my medic. Somehow he resisted and they took a pistol and shot him in the head. It's the loudest damn pistol shot I have ever heard."

The enemy then departed to rob other dead men.

Once the area immediately around them had quieted down, Kroah whispered to Conway, "Can you get up?"

"Yeah."

"Get your butt up, get back into the perimeter, and get me a radio so I can talk to Johnnie [Libs]."

Conway crawled off into the darkness. He did not return to the lieutenant that night. Kroah waited in the dark. He expected to bleed to death. He waited for a radio. He waited for death.

Then he heard a sound, someone whispering, "Hello, anybody there?" At first, Kroah would not respond. He was not sure if the voice was American. The voice grew louder as a figure emerged from deeper shadows.

"Who are you?" Kroah asked, as he could hear that it was not his radioman.

"Carpenter," came the response. An American. It was Wesley Carpenter from Kroah's platoon, Corey's fire team.

"Have you been hit?" Kroah asked.

"No, a tree fell on me."[§]

Carpenter, though hampered by swollen hands where a bullet had struck his rifle butt, shattering it and reverberating into his hands, grabbed a pair of socks from his pack and used them as makeshift bandages for Kroah's open wounds. Once the GI had done what he could to stanch the bleeding from Kroah's worst wounds the lieutenant commanded: "Find me a radio."

Carpenter obliged, crawling off and later returning with a working radio.

While Kroah waited for Carpenter to return, Ken Mize of 1st Platoon, the soldier from Arkansas who had felt relief at being wounded because he had known a bullet was going to get him eventually, spotted Leonardus Inkelaar lying outside the perimeter. Mize crawled to Inkelaar and pulled the unconscious soldier back into the perimeter. Once back within American lines, Mize could see that Inkelaar was in shock. Inkelaar's jaw and neck were so grotesquely swollen he could not manage to say "Mize." The name came out "my." Inkelaar's arm was bloody, shot up, but Mize saw that Inkelaar had "John-Wayned a tourniquet with his teeth and his good hand" around his blasted arm sometime during his ordeal.

Around the perimeter, troopers noticed that the incoming small arms fire had almost stopped. They waited for a final assault that did not come. The artillery barrage had broken up the guerillas' attempts to mass for a big push. It is also possible that the shouts through the megaphones that warned the Americans of the coming attack were theatrical instead of practical. Since the enemy's regimental commander had followed many of the standard Vietcong tactics in executing the fight that day, the possibility that he always intended to order his unit to disengage at nightfall was quite natural. The shouts of an impending attack could have been a ruse to keep the Americans off-balance, unaware of the enemy battalion's actual designs. The Army's official narrative of the battle refers to the shouts as directions for the snipers to get out of the trees to reinforce the coming attack. Perhaps so, or possibly the VC commander was withdrawing his troops in a way that would not alert the Americans to the move.[143] While Charlie Company prepared itself to battle the VC, the enemy used the time to vanish down the jungle trails.

It is also possible that the shouted orders over the megaphones were precisely what they seemed to be, and only the timely and accurate delivery of artillery on the battlefield saved the Americans. Just as the company had been mauled in the fight, the VC force must have been reeling from some genuine hurt. The following day Sergeant Charles Urconis, in an attempt to understand what had happened to the company, explored the positions held by the enemy during the fight. He spotted blood smears on the bushes and bloodstains in the trees.[144] On April 12, the American units that pursued the vanished enemy would follow obvious blood trails through the jungle. The Army estimated that upwards of 150 Vietcong were killed during the battle.[145] However, the official history of the 5th Vietcong Division as presented in Warren Wilkins' examination of enemy tactics in the early stages of the war puts the number of their dead at 41.[146] To compensate for overestimates of enemy killed from both sides, it might be appropriate to reduce by half the Army's flawed method of determining enemy dead, knocking the number down from 150 to 75.

An attempt to bulldoze Company C was out of the question for the VC commander, Dang Ngoc Si. His forces had been rapped too severely for that. He took his substantial victory and escaped while the opportunity remained. The fight, if not the night, was over.[147]

The American survivors had no way of knowing this. Though the firing had essentially died off, the men had readied themselves for a fight to the death. While waiting for this fight to develop, men began to awaken to the needs of those around them. The healthy began to aid the wounded. Mize teamed up with Pfc Dan R. Atkinson and crawled from position to position, providing first aid. Mize's and Atkinson's assistance seemed so expert to the hurt and scared soldiers that the wounded mistook them for medics and referred to them as "doc," the inevitable sobriquet for aidmen.

Five-time wounded Lieutenant Kroah, out beyond the perimeter among the 3rd Platoon dead, was finally receiving help. Using the radio retrieved by Wes Carpenter, Kroah called Libs in the clear, not worrying about call signs.

"Kroah, I thought you were dead!" a relieved Lieutenant Libs said over the radio.

"I need somebody to come out here and patch me up."

"Hold on and I'll get someone out right away."

Platoon Sergeant Charles Urconis expected to die. He did not want to die, but he expected to die. The situation was just that bad. When Libs called Urconis on the radio, the sergeant had a clip in his rifle and another clip clenched in his teeth. "I told myself I was going to take ten of them before they got me."

Libs' call meant Urconis' personal Armageddon had to wait; the Lieutenant wanted Urconis to go out and find Kroah. "Take whatever you have and go out and get Kroah."

Urconis told him, "I don't have anything but a pair of old dirty socks!"

That was enough for Libs. Urconis thought the mission was suicide, but since he told himself he should have already been dead, whether he was killed inside the perimeter or outside made little difference. He walked out into the darkness. Urconis' call signal for communications was "Oscar 5." Lieutenant Kroah's call signal was "November 6." Out among the dead, Urconis repeatedly called out, "November 6—Oscar 5," until Kroah responded.

Urconis found Kroah and Carpenter. Urconis looked over Kroah's wounds and took the pair of dirty socks, and as Carpenter had done before him, the sergeant used them like a bandage to stop the flow of blood from the lieutenant's wounds.

Urconis asked Carpenter to help him carry Kroah back to the perimeter.

"I can't, he's too big." The 110-pound Carpenter explained; holding up his swollen useless hands. Urconis knew that he could not drag Kroah back to safety by himself. He turned toward the perimeter and headed back for help.

Minutes later, the word passed through the perimeter that volunteers were needed to go outside the perimeter and retrieve a wounded lieutenant. Roger Harris, the youngest member of Charlie Company, the kid who had nailed the sniper who was making life miserable for so many near the CP, said he would go. He left his radio with Lieutenant DeVoe.[148]

Machine gunner John Noyce and Milton Lader also volunteered. Urconis, Harris, Noyce, and Lader gathered some long branches together and stretched a poncho between the wood. Harris recalls;

"Four of us…moved into the direction where 3rd platoon had been and got into an area that had been chopped down by artillery. One of our flares…popped overhead and lit us up. I thought we would…be shot down if any VC…were still in the area."[149]

The four GIs found Kroah and lifted him onto the stretcher. As they hauled the stretcher over the blasted landscape, Kroah threatened his rescuers, "If you hurt me I'll call you to attention." Kroah remembers calling cadence as the men carried him. Noyce recalled the lieutenant was babbling, and Lader laughingly remembers Kroah cursing at all of them. The four men made it back to the perimeter, and Lieutenant Kroah, five times wounded, was propped against a tree. Trooper Noyce provided a cigarette for the lieutenant.

In the same area, Pfcs Mize and Atkinson continued to tend to the wounded. One soldier prone on the ground moaned to Mize that his back was causing him fits. Mize looked him over but could only find a small wound on the GI's arm. "Man, my back is killing me," he kept saying. Finally, Mize told the GI to sit up: "Maybe that will help."

"I can't move."

Mize gently got his arm beneath the man and felt a massive hole in the back. An exit wound.

"You don't need to sit up," Mize told the soldier.

"I have to sit up," the soldier pleaded.

Against his better judgment, Mize helped prop the doomed American against a tree.

The battle was over, but no one on the U.S. side knew it. Everyman on the perimeter was ready for another assault. Most of these men were resolved to die. They pointed their weapons toward the nightmare darkness and watched the crazy shadows created by the flares floating down from C 130 Air Force gunships. The wounded suffered. Some died, bleeding to death quietly or calling out for water or their mothers or God. As the longest night of their lives bled out, some of these GIs fell asleep among their dead comrades.

---

*Pitsenbarger was posthumously awarded the nation's second-highest Air Force decoration, the Air Force Cross. It took thirty-four years before Airman First Class William H. Pitsenbarger was awarded the Medal of Honor for his actions that day. Charlie Company veterans like Fred Navarro were instrumental in seeing that Pitsenbarger received the nation's highest military honor. The people of Pitsenbarger's hometown, Piqua, Ohio, also banded together to gain recognition for their native son. Historian W. Parker Hayes contacted veterans of Pitsenbarger's Pararescue unit – Henry J. O'Beirne, Harold Salem, and others, and together these people documented Pitsenbarger's actions so that his Air Force Cross was upgraded to the Medal of Honor. The story of how Charlie Company veterans assisted in recognition for Pits is the subject of the movie; *The Last Full Measure*, written and directed by Todd Robinson.

±Company B, 2/16, had been ordered to move toward Charlie Company's position when the Vietcong had renewed their attack. Still, Bravo had subsequently halted at sunset because 2nd battalion headquarters became concerned that Charlie Company would open up on them if they approached during the night. The decision essentially sentenced Company C to defense by artillery until dawn would provide enough light to protect B Company from jittery Charlie Company trigger fingers.

**This may have been Leroy Tousant of the 1st platoon who had been wounded early in the battle, but this is only a guess.

‡Bishop survived the battle. It is unknown whether he ever had to use that .45 during the night.

§Leroy Love, also of the 3rd platoon later verified that Wesley Carpenter had been pinned beneath a huge tree branch during the first artillery barrage.

Chapter Seven:
The Mornings After

"The next morning I saw Danny Walden. Walden had little feet, I saw his little feet sticking out from under the poncho."

Ken Mize

"I found Langston. He was pretty chewed up. I cried I'm not ashamed to admit. I got pretty emotional."

Pete Faberski

"For years this (the battle) was a dream. It couldn't have happened to me. It was a dream and that's where I put it. Years later I stepped out on my patio and I smelled that smell, that smell of diesel fuel and death and it's all around me…when I came to I was in a bayou, flat on my stomach, I'm just lying there, back in that mode again."

Richard Garner

Pfc John Babino felt alone on the morning of April 12, 1966. Babino, a Brooklyn boy, was from Sergeant Navarro's squad of 3rd Platoon. On April 11, the rifleman had witnessed his squad's apocalypse: Navarro's wounding, the assault, and soldiers dropping all around him. That was why during the long dark hours of the morning of April 12 Babino felt alone and lonely; he did not think anyone besides him remained alive in his squad.

His despair peaked during the late afternoon of April 11. Babino and another soldier were lying side-by-side, putting down a base of fire. Babino momentarily felt surprisingly good about his situation. Both he and the other GI had a clear field of fire; Babino thought that together they were safe. Then the hint of optimism was dissolved in the strangled whispers of the man beside him. "I'm hit," the soldier gasped. Babino turned his head and saw the soldier clutching his throat, blood pouring through the man's fingers.

Babino called for a medic. The wounded soldier was struggling to breathe. Babino called again. Babino was not firing: he could only stare at the injured trooper and scream for a medic. Someone ran up and flopped down on the other side of the wounded man. Guerillas were attracted by the movement. They closed in. The ground was exploding around the trio of Americans. Babino knew it was time to seek better cover. He retreated, expecting the two other Americans to follow him. Several yards closer to the perimeter Babino turned to see how close behind him the medic (he assumed the soldier who had appeared was a medic) and the wounded GI were to his position. At that moment, a storm of killing lead converged on the two Americans who were still at Babino's original location. The Americans were chopped to pieces. From that moment until dawn on April 12, Babino felt utterly alone.

At first light, things changed for Babino and the remainder—the remains—of Charlie Company. Colonel William S. Hathaway, the 2nd Battalion 16th Regiment commander, and Captain Robert G. Canady, the battalion S3 and a former C Company commander, accompanied Company B, 2/16 as they entered the deserted VC base camp. A single shot rang out at 7 o'clock. An alert trooper from Bravo Company killed a guerilla left behind to gather information.[150]

The men of Charlie Company heard the shot. Roger Harris remembers that there was momentary panic among the company soldiers as men thought the shot signaled "a dawn assault." Dave Burris thought, "Oh my God, it's starting again." Phil Hall may have expressed the survivors' trepidation at hearing the shot best with his heartfelt, "Aw fuck!"

"Next thing I know there are people walking around," recalled Burris. Company B had cautiously linked up with C Company at 7:15 AM. The RTO Bobby Holton thought Bravo Company's arrival was the worst part of the experience for him. "You see these guys staring at you like, 'what the hell are you doing alive.' They didn't say anything, they just set up their perimeter." For Dan Kirby, the shocked expression on B Company soldiers' faces manifested on a personal level when he spotted a friend who had attended Advanced Infantry Training with him just a month earlier. The Bravo GI did not speak. He simply shook his head.

Stories like the above abound among Charlie Company survivors. In those first minutes as B Company set up their perimeter, relieving the company, the survivors of the battle began moving about, seeing the disaster's extent for the first time. The men's relief was palatable, but so was their growing anguish. Recalling the battle's worst aspect a year later, almost to a man, the answer was the morning of the 12th.

The battle itself was a nightmare, a horror that seemed endless at the time, but it had a certain unearthly quality that denied reality even as it occurred because it was a living nightmare. Soldiers let their training take over, and fear then could be ignored. Trying to survive during the battle, letting the adrenaline pump, and the training guide, negated the possibility of digesting the horror's magnitude. Men were too busy in the cut-and-dried business of life or death to contemplate the vagaries of war, the nasty randomness of death on the battlefield, and the guilt of simply being alive when so many were dead.

The morning after was reality. Survivors were moving about for the first time in hours, in the daylight, and could now weigh the battle's toll. For thirty-five men, the toll was their lives. The equivalent of a platoon wiped out. Sergeant James Robinson, Jr. had gone down in a rage that would earn him a Medal of Honor. Airman First Class William Pitsenbarger had diligently performed his duty—and more—until shot down. Lieutenant Charles Steinberg died leading a charge. Sergeants like Langston, Gerald, Coleman, and Seasholtz had been doing the grunt work, the non-com work when they had been killed in their myriad ways. And the grunts themselves? Men such as loner Charles Oglesby, amiable Edward Reilly, jolly Eugene Garrett, and baby-faced but dependable Randall "Peanuts" Prinz? Some died in the first moments of combat, blown to bits, or with their lives quickly snapped by a sniper's bullet. Some died slowly, wounded out beyond the perimeter, calling for water or their mothers or friends. Some were killed by Vietnamese women who stole among the bodies and eliminated any wounded they discovered. The dead ranged in age from eighteen to forty-seven, with most in their early twenties. Some were known by everyone from their platoon, a kid like Randall Prinz—3rd Platoon's unofficial mascot—or a dependable and respected non-com like Richard Manley. Others were so new, like Philyaw Fee and Carl Dwayne Buckley, that no one knew them when their bodies showed up among the dead.

The bodies were found scattered throughout the perimeter, but mainly in 3rd and 4th platoons' sectors. Platoon Sergeant Hugh Sutterfield directed Sergeant Pete Faberski to see how their friend Sergeant Langston of the 3rd Platoon had fared. Faberski found a body that was "badly chewed up," but he told himself it was Sergeant Schoolman. "Godamnit, Schoolman got killed!" Faberski said to a soldier standing beside him.

"No, no that's not Schoolman. Schoolman's over there." The soldier responded, pointing away from the body.

Schoolman, several feet away and sitting against a tree, lifted his hand in a wave. "Still here," the gesture indicated.

"Who's this?" Asked Faberski, his dread rising.

"That's Langston." And Faberski broke down.

Helicopters dropped engineers into the jungle. The engineers were equipped with chainsaws. As the men of the company moved about the battlefield, the engineers hacked out a landing zone large enough for a big Chinook helicopter to land. Several landed that day to take away the wounded and the dead.

Later in the morning, Airman First Class Henry O'Beirne, expecting to find his friend A1C William Pitsenbarger alive on the ground, was told that Pitsenbarger was dead. This revelation was a shock because, during the night, the pararescue crew had been assured he was still alive. Pitsenbarger's body was uncovered so that O'Beirne could positively identify the remains. The saddened pararescue man counted four wounds on the body.[151]

Pfc John Noyce helped recover bodies throughout the morning. What struck him as particularly telling about the ferocity of the battle and the expert positioning of the enemy's guns were the locations of some of the 4th Platoon's bodies. Sergeant William Causey, Specialist 4 Charles Oglesby, Sergeant Coleman, and others who attempted to follow Lieutenant Steinberg in his assault on the .51 caliber machine gun were located sprawled in a line. Cut down as neatly as a row of corn. The machine-gun fire had cut through the Americans in an unstoppable arc.

Roger Harris was also out in the jungle recovering bodies. He came across one stiff body lying face down in the dirt and blood. Harris rolled the body over; the corpse needed to be bagged. The youngest member of Charlie Company was relieved that he did not know the soldier, but he reminded himself that there were other bodies in other bags that he did know.[152]

Ken Mize, though wounded himself, was compelled to assess the damage. He wandered about the perimeter until he found himself looking down at the accumulating rows of poncho-covered bodies. Without removing the ponchos, Mize realized that Danny Walden had been killed, just as Walden had predicted would happen. "Walden had little feet, I saw his little feet sticking out from under the poncho."

RTO Bobby Holton was too tired, too heart-sick to pull himself away from the rows of bodies. An Associated Press photographer, one of many news people haunting the battleground that morning, snapped Holton's photo sitting on a tree stump. Holton's weapon in his hands—the rifle butt on the ground staring at "the long lines of bags containing the bodies of his dead mates…"

Another photo taken that morning shows a grainy picture of three-body bags and a helmet, all lying on the jungle floor. Two of the body bags are in the background; one is in the foreground, next to the helmet. Blood in the form of black spots is visible on the body bag. The helmet has the words, "the Barber SAID,

NEXT" scrawled across the helmet. The caption below the photo read in part, "The helmet...rests on the ground next to the bloodied rubber bag encasing his body. Written in a happier moment on the camouflage canvas covering the helmet is the inscription, 'The Barber Said, Next.' The soldier was one of many...killed..."[*] The helmet belonged to Eugene Garrett, Jr. of Houston, Texas, a jovial sort whose time in-country was almost up. He had scribbled the words on his helmet to indicate how little time remained for him in Vietnam.

There was another photo or should have been, of a particularly gruesome-looking American corpse. A photographer or network cameraman had spotted the mauled corpse just before soldiers covered it with a poncho. Knowing a good picture when he saw one, the photographer had excitedly told another reporter to remove the poncho so he could take the shot. The company XO, Lieutenant Ken Alderson, heard the exchange and charged over to the photographer with his rifle leveled.

"Get out of here before I shoot you!" Alderson screamed. And that particularly gruesome image was not taken, and Ken Alderson preserved a bit of dignity for a dead man.

Then there was the living. Seventy-one of the company's survivors were wounded.[±] At least one of the wounded, Deane Van Dyke, would die from his wounds. Only twenty-eight men boarded the helicopters unscathed. The injured had to be cared for. Sergeant John Fulford, temporarily blinded after being shot in the head by a sniper, had to be guided to the helicopters. The severely wounded such as Leonardus Inkelaar and Lieutenant Kroah had to be evacuated immediately.

Rick Owens of the 2nd Platoon, who had shrapnel embedded in his neck and a bullet wound, was carrying GI corpses to the helicopters when a medic saw his condition and told him to get on the helicopter himself. For the next forty years, Owens believed that he was one of only about twenty-five American survivors of the battle.

Thirst was a problem for many of the wounded. Men had depleted their water quickly during the fight the day before. Now, these wounded, who had already bled through the night, were mad with thirst. Pfc Galen Summerlot found Doug Landry lying on the ground, his wounds oozing blood. Landry was not worried about the wounds; he was only thinking about quenching his overpowering thirst. Water was in short supply—Summerlot opened a can of peaches and offered Landry a drink of the juice. Dan Kirby would do the same for Pfc James Finney—shot in the shoulder—when Kirby came across him.

Kirby himself had been shot in the leg, but he was among the walking wounded. These men, battered and bloody—with less than life-threatening wounds, continued to move around the battlefield like punch-drunk tourists, which in a macabre way they were. One soldier came across John Lang on a stretcher among the more seriously wounded. Despite his shot-up leg, Lang intended to let others know that he had fought for Charlie Company, "I got me twelve of them Vietcong last night," he said. Lang would spend months in hospitals recovering from his wounds.

2nd Platoon's Phil Hall bagged the bodies and then assisted the wounded to the helicopters before the smell of death and war overpowered him. In Vietnam since the last days of December 1965, Hall could not help lamenting the realization that "I had eight more months of this shit."

Sergeant Sutterfield had also had enough for that day. When the swarm of high-ranking officers hit the ground (DePuy showed up and others), one general approached Sutterfield. The general had known Sutterfield for years and respected him. When the general told the sergeant that he would find him a desk job, Sutterfield, in a matter-of-fact tone, told the officer to "stuff it."

Nineteen-year-old medic Bob Fisher described the toll on the living as "...a despondence, and a separation from the rest of the world..." Each man could see it in the eyes of his fellow soldiers, "[w]e had been through the bowels of hell, and now we were emerging alive...Traces of fear could still be seen, confusion was also evident, but the look that portrayed the experience of the day was more than that. [T]he eyes projected a pain and sadness that even a picture could not capture..."

Fisher saw that look as incredibly intense in the eyes of Captain Nolen, the company commander. Fisher happened upon Nolen while the captain was speaking with the commander of Bravo Company. Fisher asked Nolen if he [Fisher] could now treat Nolen's wound. Nolen had earlier refused aid, as he had refused assistance from his RTO Gilbert Delao, but now he allowed Fisher to bandage him. Five months later, Nolen wrote to Fisher to thank him for his outstanding service on April 11th and to report that his (Nolen's) wounds had finally healed.[153]

In a CBS news report that aired in the United States the following day, journalist John Flynn began his summation of the fight outside the village of Xa Cam My with the words, "The war hasn't stopped in Vietnam and this scene should prove it." The camera work on the report was shaky and disjointed; almost as if the cameraman had been spooked by what he was filming. Disjointed perfectly matched the scenes it depicted. The camera catches a nameless trooper with his face slightly turned down. The soldier glances up. The camera captures a hint of what that soldier must have felt, for the soldier's eyes seemed crowded with fear. The scene shifts to a soldier crying into his hands. A comrade standing before the distraught GI grabbed the crying soldier by the nape of the neck and pulled him to his shoulder for just a moment. Next came shots of litter-bound wounded being carried out of the jungle to waiting helicopters. Then a grisly tableau quickly dissolves as four men carrying a body bag move beyond the camera's view, and a quick zoom brings into focus a pile of body bags just beyond where the four soldiers had stumbled with their burden.[154]

Flynn narrated, "The Vietcong were everywhere, even hanging from the trees." On the television screen: boots, turned toe down, and legs in bloused trousers (trouser legs tucked into the boots) extended out from beneath a poncho.[155] The camera had snagged a real prize; these were Airman First Class William Pitsenbarger's remains—the clean boots were the key to that gruesome identification.

There was one piece of good news transmitted unwittingly by the CBS report. One of the soldiers filmed was pictured in profile, stubble on his chin and wearing dirty fatigues like a Technicolor version of Bill Mauldin's Willie and Joe. Also revealed in that particular shot was the soldier's helmet, and on the helmet was scrawled the name "Carol Kozial."[156] A father in the states caught the report and was happy to see that particular name written on the helmet. The father knew Carol Kozial because his son, Milton Lader, had been dating Carol since high school. When CBS's report flashed in Mr. Lader's living room in Portsmouth, Virginia, that afternoon in April, and the senior Lader saw that the trooper wearing that particular helmet was alive, he knew that his son was safe.

Another Virginia family with a boy in Charlie Company was not as lucky. Roger Harris writes of what happened when the family saw the report on CBS;

> "My father had put in nine hours in the...factory and [was sitting] in his living room to listen to the news.... The anchor started with the report that an...infantry company of

the Big Red One, C Company, 2nd of 16th Infantry, had been nearly wiped out.... My father could not hold back the tears as he went to my friends' homes for several days to find someone who may have heard from me."[157]

These were agonizing days, not-knowing days, dreadful days. The news would finally be good for the Harris family. Roger had survived the Battle of Xa Cam My (the battle has also been referred to as the Second Battle of the Courtenay Plantation. The Vietnamese know it as the Battle of Tam Bo, for the stream that flowed nearby.)

Toward the end of the report, the correspondent accurately stated that "there's not much left of Charlie Company." He could have ended with that bit of sad news, but instead, the closing words of the report were, "And the survivors will have a lot of memories."[158]

..

The memories lurked in the back of the survivors' minds and most of the men simply suppressed them or fled them. Wes Carpenter was sent to the hospital for his busted-up hands and his strained back, (recall that a huge tree limb from an artillery burst had flattened him early in the battle) soon the doctors declared him fit. What he needed most was not medical care but to erase the memories of that nightmare on the rubber plantation. The Army offered him a thirty-day leave for Guam, but Carpenter told the higher-ups he had a wife back in the states and she was the only rest and recreation he needed. He was informed that he could go home if he could find a flight out of South Vietnam and still be back in thirty days. Carpenter made his way to Saigon and hitched a ride on the first plane heading to the U.S. He found himself on a C-130 Hercules. He was packed in a small, curtained compartment with a few other

GIs at the tail end of the plane, all facing backward, toward the rear ramp. Carpenter was a smoker and could not make the duration of the flight without a cigarette. The other GIs told him he would have to move to the front of the plane to smoke. Standing up, Carpenter turned toward the cockpit and pulled aside the curtain that had shielded the remainder of the plane's cargo from view. There, stretching out to the front of the plane were coffins carrying dead GIs home. He just could not escape the dead of Vietnam.

For some, the memories involved healing and getting through traumatic months in military hospitals. John Lang spent so much time in the hospital from his torn-up leg that he collected a kiss from Ann-Margret when she traveled to Vietnam for the 1966 Bob Hope Christmas Special. Lang had missed the actress when she had encountered the company in late March of 1966 on a guided tour to encourage soldiers actually out in the field. Lang had been envious of his comrades who had seen her then, but in the hospital he had her to himself for the few seconds it took her to peck him on the forehead. Dan Kirby was in the hospital in Zama, Japan, for four months with what doctors told him was a million-dollar wound—a back-to-America wound. He was misinformed. One day while still recovering from the bullet wound, Kirby was told he was heading back to Vietnam. He requested that he be sent back to Company C. In Charlie Company, he might know some people.

Kirby did not recognize as many faces as he perhaps thought he would. 3rd Platoon had been decimated in the battle; the men he saw were new. However, because most of these replacements had arrived en masse to replace the dead and wounded from April 11th four months earlier, they thought of themselves as old hands and Kirby as the newbie. Kirby did find Galen Summerlot of the 2nd Platoon. Summerlot and Kirby had gone through Advanced Infantry Training together. They had arrived in Vietnam and been assigned to the company within days of one another. These two and other survivors of April 11, 1966, would spend the remainder of their tour sure that another day like "that day," lurked within every day in Vietnam.

Kirby and Summerlot, Steve Antal of 2nd Platoon, Harold Hunter of 4th Platoon, Dave Burris of 3rd Platoon, and the other survivors of that day who had been wounded but sent back to the unit did not talk about it. None of the new men asked the survivors about the battle, and none of the survivors spoke among themselves about it. They stored away those memories. Memories that would turn into nightmares; could turn into Post Traumatic Stress Disorder and other ailments related to their time in Vietnam.

Some men in the hospitals had received million-dollar wounds – if they wanted them. Lieutenant Marty Kroah had been punctured in so many ways during the battle that he could return home for the asking. He did not have to return to complete his tour of duty. But Kroah was career Army and an officer. He volunteered to spend another year in Vietnam later in the war, so he ended up roaming the Mekong Delta fighting drug use among his men as much as he fought the Vietcong. Kroah's memories came in the form of guilt. Even after decades of mulling it over, Kroah could come to no other conclusion about the friendly fire artillery at the beginning of the battle than that he was responsible for calling in the wrong coordinates that brought those killing shells down on the company's position.

Sergeant John Fulford was not permanently blinded despite being shot in the eye. He lost sight in one eye and required corrective surgery for the other, but he did achieve limited vision in one eye. Leonardus Inkelaar, the GI who had his arm torn up, his jaw broken, and three vertebrae cracked, spent three months in a military hospital in the Philippines and then more time at Ft. Riley, Kansas, for rehabilitation. At the end of 1966, with his rehabilitation complete, the Army invited Inkelaar to re-enlist. He considered it, but when he asked how soon he would have to go back to Vietnam, he was told "immediately." The Army wanted him to complete the tour of duty that had been interrupted by the events of April 11. Inkelaar refused. James Finney did go home because of his shoulder wound. His Vietnam War lasted seven days. There were many others like Fulford, Inkelaar, and Finney. They were wounded. They were treated, and if they did not see fit to re-enlist, they were ushered back into civilian life. And the memories, sometimes masquerading as nightmares, festered.

Even those men who received minor wounds or no wounds at all had their share of memories/nightmares from the battle. Twenty-eight men were in this category, twenty-eight out of the 134 Charlie Company soldiers who had walked into the Courtenay Rubber Plantation ambush. The rest were dead or wounded. The healthy still had obligations to Uncle Sam. They had a war to fight, and after replacements brought the unit back to full strength, the men of Charlie Company began patrolling again. There was the frightened sergeant who had threatened Pete Faberski when Faberski had tried to prod him back into the fight. After the battle, this non-com pulled patrols and did his duty and contemplated his actions from April 11 until the day in June when he drown crossing a river. There was Faberski himself, who finished his couple of months remaining in-country and then flew back to the states only to find himself warily eyeing the tree line surrounding the American airport where he once again touched U.S. soil. The terrors were everywhere. Faberski half expected to see the flash of green tracers from every tree line. He was also career Army and would spend another year in Vietnam later in the war. His nightmares centered around the death of his friend Everett Eugene "Round

Man" Langston, and Faberski let them remain nightmares rather than deal with the horror.

Roger Harris grew up on April 11, 1966. He was an eighteen-year-old kid who had seen too much death. His nightmares made him ask himself why he had survived the battle while many of his friends had not. His answer came, to his satisfaction, in 1990 with the birth of his son. These men, Harris, Faberski, and the sergeant who drown, represent the men who survived without acquiring physical scars but carried the memories/nightmares within.

Then there were the extreme cases. These men suffered from and lived with chronic Post Traumatic Stress Disorder. One survivor had gone to Vietnam as a gentle young man but emerged after two years there as a denizen of the night, seeking solitude in the darkness, seeking escape in violence. This veteran had not died Xa Cam My and so for years pursued that goal in the United States. Like Roger Harris, only the birth of a child would save the man. There was Steve Antal, who became a farmer. Haunted by memories too vivid, too personal, he lives in Indiana, but his mind is always in Vietnam. Ron Haley is another veteran of the battle who has dealt with painful memories by destroying them. Upon returning to the safety of America, he was a man who chose the dangerous life of an outlaw biker. A rebel on two wheels, he did not pose the part; he became it, a true one-percenter. For Haley, the battle only appeared in flashes, horrifying glimpses that left him breathless and shaking. The motorcycles were simply a way to outrun those terrifying memories. There are too many Charlie Company veterans like these three.

There are flashbacks for all the men, the well-adjusted, and the others. Some are just hints rather than full-blown flashbacks. Dave Burris, the point man on April 11, 1966, spent time decades after the battle walking in the wooded mountains of California's Coastal Range just west of Silicon Valley. The walks were pleasant strolls with his wife. Peaceful walks. Yet, when the sun came knifing through the Redwood branches at just the right angle, April 11th crept over Burris, raising the hairs on the back of his neck and shattering the walk so sharply that the woods were no longer lovely, no longer friendly, no longer peaceful. Instead, he was reminded of the haunting darkness and hints of sunlight among the trees of the Courtenay Rubber Plantation of Phuoc Tuy Province.

Some flashbacks are full-blown frightful attacks like those suffered by Richard Garner of Shreveport, Louisiana. Wounded during the battle, Garner spent months in hospitals before he was able to return home. Upon arrival at the Oakland Airport, he was verbally accosted by young people who called him various unsavory names. Yes, Garner was that prototypical GI who returned from the Vietnam War accused of being a baby killer. Except this baby killer was incapacitated as he arrived in Oakland, too weak to defend himself from the college students' misinformed taunts. But he endured.

Garner did more than endure. He recovered. He started a new life, a life denuded of Vietnam. He got on with his life as everyone told him to do. It worked or seemed to. But those memories, those nightmares were churning somewhere down in Richard Garner's subconscious, and one day decades after his Vietnam War had ended, it all came rushing back:

> "For years this (the battle) was a dream. It couldn't have happened to me. It was a dream and that's where I put it. Years later I stepped out on my patio and I smelled that smell, that smell of diesel fuel and death and it's all around me...when I came to I was in a bayou, flat on my stomach, I'm just laying there, back in that mode again."

A year or two later, while visiting the Houston Medical Center to treat a rare form of cancer, Garner had another episode. For three days, his motel room off of Interstate 10 was the Courtenay Rubber Plantation's fetid jungles. He was again in danger of being killed. The nightmares had claimed him. These memories, these nightmares, have not defeated Richard Garner, but where once he thought he had vanquished them, now he knows they will be with him until his last day.

The reporter's, John Flynn, words, "And the survivors will have a lot of memories," were more than a catchy way to end a news story. It was a curse on the survivors of the Battle of Xa Cam My.

..

In a chapter entitled "Keep an Eye on the Ball," which appears in the book *Infantry in Vietnam*, the author, Captain Robert E. Ward, III, takes the Charlie Company commander to task for failing to send out patrols during the air evacuation stage of the battle. Ward writes, "The encirclement could probably have been prevented by active patrolling on all sides of the perimeter during the company's halt."[159] Ward had lauded the company's actions in "tracking the enemy and keeping him in its sights" early in the day but then criticized the commander during the medical evacuation process: "Company C...took its eyes off the ball, permitting the enemy to maneuver undetected into attack positions around a hastily formed perimeter." Ward writes that the fight from that point was "...a complete surprise to Company C...."[160]

Ward was a battalion staff officer and had worked on the after-action report and the unit citation for valorous action. Ken Alderson, the company executive officer who had endured the fight, believed that by writing the chapter, a "lessons learned" piece for *Infantry* magazine, Ward had left out some details that would have better explained the situation. Alderson and John Libs, 2nd Platoon's commander, both believed that by the time the medical evacuations got underway, the company knew the Vietcong were out beyond the perimeter—that was why they created a perimeter! There was no need for active patrolling, as Ward suggested. Small groups of men wandering outside a perimeter would have allowed those men to be picked off easily, weakening the unit and not materially contributing to its defense. "We would have been piecemealed," Alderson asserted. "We knew we were going to get hit." This was the gist of Alderson and Libs' argument.

Alderson believed another of Ward's statements was more important to understanding the battle's outcome. Ward had written, "Reinforcements should have been readily available, too, or the companies within the battalion should have been mutually supporting—no more than an hour apart under the most adverse conditions."[161] The crux of the situation for Alderson. Company B had been too far away from Charlie Company to get through the jungle in time to blunt the attack.

More than two decades later, General William DePuy, the division commander at the time of the battle, acknowledged in a letter to John Libs that the companies operating in the vicinity of the Courtenay Rubber Plantation on April 11, 1966, had been too far apart. He called it a "lesson learned at great cost."[162]

According to author George Wilson in *Mud Soldiers*, Bravo Company 2/16 was a thousand meters away when the fighting started just after noon.[163] R. P. Harrison of B Company, 2/18 thought the distances were more like six hundred meters.[164] Either way, it was more than the four hundred meters that were recommended for practical support.

Alderson also believed that even a seasoned company commander would have been hard-pressed to do much more than was done that afternoon. Certainly, Nolen was inexperienced—he had been advised to listen to Alderson and Libs—and following the initial contact and the misdirected artillery response, he did not possess the combat savvy to influence the fight forcefully. The early friendly fire and deadly contact had Alderson and Libs advising Nolen to establish a perimeter so that the dead and wounded could be evacuated. Because the artillery fire had gone awry and slammed into Charlie Company positions, General DePuy had temporarily suspended artillery support.** With no artillery support available, Nolen could have called for infantry support. Or perhaps the battalion commander should have made that call. No one did.

Many in the unit had thought the fight was over after the initial contact. 1st Platoon's Lieutenant Smith DeVoe commented on that phase of the battle: "I thought it was over. Everyone did." If Nolen also believed that the fight was finished, he would not have called in infantry support. Alderson and Libs had been in Vietnam for months, and nothing that occurred early in the battle triggered a desire for reinforcements. Getting some kind of landing zone established to evacuate the wounded was the primary concern by the time the enemy struck their most brutal blow.

The After-Action Report pointed out that Intelligence reports warned that the Vietcong would strike if they believed they had "achieved tactical surprise as well as numerical superiority" and that the guerillas would "defend his base areas with the forces immediately available to him..."[165] Furthermore, the same intelligence reports remarked that the enemy had had years to build defenses in depth (an exaggeration but the position had been prepared for battle.) When Charlie Company stumbled across those jungle trails and followed those subterranean soldiers spotted by Lieutenant Kroah's RTO, they were already doomed.

The VC commander knew the location of the supporting units, and the company's strength and knew how he wanted the battle to unfold. The friendly fire mishap was a lucky break for the Vietcong but not the deciding factor in attacking the company. When the Americans laagered-up to evacuate the wounded, the enemy leader waited to see if the other American units would move to Charlie Company's aid. Perhaps the commander had even set out ambushes for any American reinforcements. As the afternoon progressed and no other units moved in the company's direction, the guerilla commander ordered an attack on the Americans as the GIs were busy trying to get their wounded buddies on helicopters. The attack's timing was also a typical Vietcong tactic, coming close to nightfall so that after the guerillas had mauled the company, they could drift back into the jungle.

Another consideration when attempting to explain what happened to Company C on April 11, 1966, is to remember the tactics employed by the American Army at that time. High-ranking field officers, such as 3rd Brigade's Colonel William D. Brodbeck, had recognized the Vietcong's ability to avoid the American large unit area sweeps. The officers could not bring the enemy to blows because the guerillas were choosing when to fight. The enemy decided to fight only when they believed they could win by shocking an isolated American unit. Brodbeck and other officers began breaking down their sweeps "into platoon and company-size patrols to lure them [Vietcong] into attacking."[166] Colonel A. E. Milloy, commanding 2nd Brigade at the time of ABILENE, must have approved of Brodbeck's strategy because Companies A, B, and C 2/16, and B 2/18 were each deployed in such a way as to present themselves as ripe targets for the enemy on April 11, 1966. However, Milloy must have believed he could quickly shuttle aid to any unit that came under attack.

General DePuy later denied that he had dangled Charlie Company as bait. In his 1988 letter to John Libs, DePuy wrote that he had "[o]nly once... put out a unit for bait – on the Minh Thanh road...."[167] Whether a reader accepts DePuy's assertion may depend on how a reasonable person wants to interpret the word 'bait." In the operation that culminated in the Battle of the Minh Thanh Road on July 9, 1966, a specific unit was designated the bait, and all other units were geared to rapidly pounce on any enemy units that might strike at the "bait." This particular operation included leaking the decoy unit's location and supposed mission to questionable South Vietnamese sources so that the enemy would hear of the tempting target.[168] That unit was "bait," and the entire operation was based on using such a decoy.

On the other hand, in operations such as ABILENE, where companies were sent out on search-and-destroy missions, there were no attempts at deception. No single unit acted as the designated bait; these units, though not so designated, were deployed in a manner that military planners hoped would lure the Vietcong into striking, which would then allow the Americans' supporting artillery to crush the enemy. Any company stomping through the jungles of Phuoc Tuy Province on April 11, 1966, was a target. Each had an equal chance of being hit by the watching enemy. It was a matter of luck—or more aptly, lack of luck—as to which company would be attacked. The military acknowledged the risks in such tactics, but if the ploy resulted in the Army engaging the enemy, the chances were considered worth taking. Charlie Company was just the unlucky unit that stumbled too close to the enemy's base camp.

If DePuy's understanding (rationalization) of the meaning of "bait" in the context of American use of tactics in Vietnam— that essentially only when a specific unit had been designated for the role of "bait" and had an entire operation built around tricking the enemy into pouncing on that "bait"—is accepted, Charlie Company's travail on Easter Monday 1966 was not a result of the company being offered as an enticement for the enemy to show themselves. However, if the division's *de facto* standard operating procedure for search and destroy operations during the spring of 1966 is recognized for what it was, then Company C, like companies A and B 2/16 and B 2/18, was bait.

In *Mud Soldiers,* George Wilson relates a confrontation between a tired, angry Lieutenant Libs and General DePuy. DePuy had flown onto the battlefield on April 12 to see the damage. This conversation seems to confirm that the company, like all the companies in the operation, was being used as a lure:

"'You put us out there as bait.' [said Libs.] DePuy sat silent. Libs knew he had gotten through to the general.

'You walked us into a goddamn holocaust, General.'

'Yeah, but there's no other way to get a goddamn fight going,' DePuy replied.

'Well you got one going here.'"[169]

..

The letter DePuy wrote to Libs more than twenty years after the battle also carries DePuy's admission that the officers "...did a poor job at the command level (Div, brigade, and battalion) and Company C paid its [the command's] enormous price."[170] However, as the conversation between DePuy and Libs showed and as DePuy stated in his letter to Libs, it was the company's and the entire /Army's job to fight the enemy. "[W]e were looking for and hoping for contact because that was our job."

A job. Find the enemy and pile on. Yet, the enemy would not let the Army do its job in the first months of 1966. The enemy had learned to avoid the big lumbering American units searching for them. The enemy would not attack these behemoths who could stomp them. For example, Wes Carpenter had been in-country since January yet had seen no action until the 11th of April, though he had heard tales about some lethal mishaps with water buffalo from his comrades. The enemy would not fight the American Army's war. So, the American Army, whose job it was to demolish the enemy, sought to feign fighting the Vietcong's war. The Americans allowed units to *appear* to become isolated so that the enemy would strike; then, the Americans would do their job and annihilate them.

Such tactics were chancy because, through a miscalculation, a misunderstood order, or other human error, American soldiers could become isolated in fact, not appearance. These tactics were risky because they allowed the Vietcong to continue to initiate contact and to decide when and where to fight. The Americans were not just feigning fighting the guerillas' war; once shots were fired and blood spilled, they were fighting it for real.

It may be that some things went wrong on April 11, 1966. The fact that the company commander was new and less than martial in outlook did not help the situation, but neither does it explain it. The friendly fire created chaos among green troops and old hands alike but had been dealt with before the major part of the battle commenced. That patrols were not sent out during the medical evacuation period probably saved lives rather than being responsible for causing deaths. Even the fact that the company, like all companies that day, was being used as bait does not explain the cause of the defeat. The out-of-place supporting companies were a factor—no help available to Charlie Company meant that the enemy commander could execute his plan without regard to the other American units—but that was not the deciding factor in this American defeat.

What decided the fight in the VC's favor was that Charlie Company, the 2nd Brigade, the First Infantry Division, and the American Army, were all fighting the Vietcong's war. The illusion existed that the Army had come up with a way to deal with the guerillas, lure them in, and then pound them into the ground, but this tactic ignored what was already common knowledge about the enemy's leadership; namely that the guerillas controlled the rate of casualties among their forces.[171] If they chose to fight, it was because the commander on the spot had weighed the probable cost of attacking the Americans. The leader of the attacking regiment, Dang Ngoc Si, could not know that the first artillery barrage would do more damage to Charlie Company than to his forces. Far more likely is the idea that the guerilla leader had expected heavier casualties than he initially took in attacking the company. Heavy casualties would have been the expected price for mauling the Americans—the price for victory.

Victory is how the Vietcong viewed the fight on April 11, 1966. The enemy had avoided the Americans during ABILENE until Dang Ngoc Si could sense an opportunity for victory.[172] Then he struck, and though he lost between forty to eighty soldiers, he had handed the Americans a defeat.

---

*The writing on the helmet is pictured as I have quoted, the first two words with the first letters capitalized, the other letters in those words in lowercase, while the remaining words are in all capital letters. See the photo section.

±Many others, such as Bob Fisher and Charles Urconis, had been wounded but considered the wounds so minor that they ignored them.

**DePuy told Kroah this information after the battle while the lieutenant was in the hospital. Kroah was in no mood to coddle the general. Kroah blurted out, "What idiot stopped the artillery?" (this is the sanitized version). DePuy informed Kroah that he was the idiot.

DePuy may have ordered the artillery stopped until the GT (Gun to Target) lines could be cleared up, or the General assumed responsibility for the snafu to allow Kroah to vent. DePuy and other men up the chain of command seemed genuinely distressed by Charlie Company's fate.

Epilogue:
The Reunion, 2001

"We kicked their ass!"

A cry from numerous Charlie Company veterans during the First Charlie Company Reunion, Nashville, Tennessee, July 2001.

The brochure proclaimed the establishment was "newly remodeled" and "clean." The reality was old and dirty. The accommodations were a motel in Nashville. A national hotel chain in a neglected location that must have relied heavily on the naïve trade, parents coming to visit their Vanderbilt University freshmen for the first time, or cut-rate country music fans needing only a place to flop between trips to the Grand Ole Opry. The white two-story stucco building—two structures with a parking lot between them—was jammed against a busy avenue, so road noise was abundant, and entering or exiting the parking lot in an automobile required the skills of a Richard Petty. Still, it was cheap and within easy driving distance of the swank Renaissance Nashville Hotel downtown where the 1st Infantry Division Association was holding its 2001 annual reunion. Charlie Company veterans had chosen to hold their first company reunion simultaneously and in the same city as the division's soirée, but at arm's length, and in a locale more attuned to some of the attendees' sensibilities.

Old and faded. Gone to seed. Seen better days. Any of these clichés defining the motel could have as aptly described a few of the Charlie Company men arriving in the July heat to rekindle friendships, shore up memories, and shed some tears. One veteran arrived early—on Wednesday—and then hung around the tiny lobby on Thursday, greeting every comrade that checked in for the first day of the reunion. This unofficial greeter sported a mullet of grey hair extending from beneath a greasy Bass Pro Shop cap to the middle of his back. A skinny kid in 1966, cadaverous, in the motel lobby he carried so many extra pounds on his belly that the polo shirt he wore could not cover all of it.

Dave Peters, arriving on Thursday afternoon, had gotten the memo. He arrived in a white polo shirt—the food stains on the front evidence of the ten-hour drive he had just completed from northern Ohio. "Get it to go and then go," he explained. His hair was long and mostly grey.

Then a veteran arrived fresh. Trim. And with a pretty young brunette on his arm. His toupee was drastically black, as was his beard. This veteran was good-natured about the toupee, lifting the front as if he were doffing his hat. He introduced the brunette as his fiancée to the overly interested Charlie Company veterans. She was a find, her low-cut dress exposing just enough of a tattoo in the cleavage to make the other veterans envious of their comrade. She seemed uninterested in the proceedings.

And on they came. Many with guts too large and shirts too tight. Hair greyed or Grecian-Formulated to a lustrous shine. Some bald. Most fiftyish fading into sixtyish. Except for the voices. These men bellowed hellos and cracked out laughter as they recognized some other warrior from the past. They embraced unashamedly, and there was a lift to the voices, a shedding of years as these men in their fifties were transported back to the glory days of their late teens and early twenties. All it took was the sight of an old friend.

They brought their wives, loyal women who, for the most part, kept their mouths shut. Some men came alone. For them, the reunion was not a sharing thing. This gathering was about something other than their present-day lives.

One veteran's wife appeared in the lobby when each veteran showed up. She was younger than most of the wives—though not so young as to rival the tattooed fiancée—and she was as loud as the men. She would scoop up the new arrivals before they had time to find their rooms. She instead steered them to the second floor where a conference room with walls decorated with hundreds of black and white vintage photographs of Charlie Company awaited them. The shouting and laughter would commence. This woman would gesture at the new arrival's wife and bring her over to a counter loaded down with beer cans and liquor bottles. Then she would disappear from the room, off to snag another arrival while the veteran was engulfed by the revelry and the just arrived veteran's wife, stranded by the liquor among other wives, began the small talk, or, looking over the room and realizing what was coming, poured themselves a stiff one.

There was no program that first night—there was no program any night, not at the motel away from the swank surroundings of the Renaissance in downtown Nashville. At the motel, the men sat in folding metal chairs at long metal tables, smoked and drank beer, and talked about the long ago. At the Renaissance, men sat in cushioned conference chairs at small circular wooden tables and drank mixed drinks, and did not smoke, for smoking was prohibited in the hotel. The motel floor was linoleum and hard—the carpet at the Renaissance was soft and absorbed noise. At the Renaissance, men looked in their brochures to make sure they were not missing a meeting of their unit's memorial services for fallen comrades; at the motel, men drifted in and out of the smoke-filled conference room as they pleased. It simply did not matter when a Charlie Company veteran entered the room or left after the initial arrival because the same conversations that had wished him farewell when he left the room were still going on in some form when he returned.

The men at the motel had been enlisted men in their day. The officers were over at the Renaissance. Marty Kroah was at the motel, but that was to be expected: Marty had always been more of an enlisted man than an officer. Marty might have risen through the ranks, but he had never felt comfortable around other officers. His place was with the enlisted.

Alderson, Libs, and Devoe each had a room at the Renaissance. Each spent far more time visiting with members of the division association than with the men in the motel. When these three did show up in that smoke-filled conference room on Friday, they stood just inside the doors, and their smiles were strained. Each was trim, well-groomed, and appeared to have aged gracefully. Only Alderson broke away from the entrance to take Pete Faberski in hand. They huddled together—but outside the room—for a few minutes. Their conversation was on a shared moment during the battle, but each remembered it differently, and so the conversation died.

These former officers stayed less than an hour. Then they made their excuses and disappeared. Their clothes would have smelled of cigarettes. They probably showered and changed before attending the association business meeting, followed by a reception and dinner in the hotel's ballroom.

Another retired officer showed up at the motel. He was trim and well-groomed like the other officers had been, but he was not among their group. His room was at the motel with the men. Ramon Padilla had captained the company for one month just before Operation ABILENE.

Padilla was charming, making a point to recall some little something about each of the men. He also wooed the wives, who must have been struck by his distinguished good looks and impeccable manners. He tended to pontificate on all subjects. He inflated his place in the company's history—after all, he had only commanded the unit for a month—but he was liked and respected by the veterans.

What the men saw in Padilla was a different outcome to the battle. If only he had been in charge that day, then things would have turned out differently, better. Padilla had been all Army when he ran the company. He had the men testing their weapons and running drills in base camp—no officer did that—and generally keeping the men sharp. He exuded confidence in his martial abilities, and that made the men confident in him. Among the veterans in Nashville that July, the thinking was that had Padilla been in charge instead of Nolen, the battle would not have been such a shambles.

No one followed up on this general feeling of confidence in Padilla by asking why he had been replaced after such a short tenure. Why had he replaced Captain Canady in the first place—who was combat savvy and had been the company commander for only six months. Padilla had a ready excuse for his removal, some sketchy story about the Philippine military's desperate need for Spanish-speaking American advisors.

Ken Alderson, who had served as the executive officer under all three commanders—Canady, Padilla, and Nolen—had a ready answer: the division had an oversupply of captains! Alderson had, like any career officer, hungered for company command. He naturally saw himself as Canady's successor. However, when Canady was promoted to a battalion staff position, HQ had bypassed Alderson, who was just a first lieutenant, and named Padilla commander. After Padilla had his taste of command and clashes with company officers and battalion staff, he was replaced by Nolen, another captain. When Nolen was wounded during the battle of April 11, Alderson was de facto commander for a few days but only long enough for the battalion staff to decide which of the other surplus captains was next to get their "ticket-punched."

Career officers recognized that, to rise in the service, command of a company during the war was a must: no combat experience, no future. The high command also recognized this. Therefore, company commanders like Canady, who had spent six months in the field learning combat conditions, were rotated out of that critical job so that another captain, in this case, Padilla, could get his "ticket-punched."

Would Padilla have made a difference that April Monday back in '66? The men at the motel thought he would have done a better job. That is why he was treated so well by those men.

By Friday night Padilla tactfully absented himself from the meeting room. The men were talking about watching "the video." The video was a pirated copy of a CBS news report of the battle. One of the veterans who had attended the 1999 Medal of Honor Award ceremony for Airman Pitsenbarger had coaxed a copy from an Air Force Museum curator. Only a handful of the men had seen the video. That Friday night, as men came in from McDonald's or the Chinese buffet down the street, each took a seat facing a television sitting on a high media stand. There was laughter and clusters of men by the liquor counter who continued to talk, but everyone knew something important was about to happen.

There was no set time to start the video. Someone just looked around, figured enough people were there, walked over to the television, and turned it on. Some wives left the room. The men by the liquor moved closer to the television. Already men like Kroah and Faberski and half-blind John Fulford were leaning in toward the television.

The screen was black at first, "it's a voiceover at first," someone said, then the narration began; "[t]he War hasn't stopped in Vietnam. And this scene should prove it." The scene is of dirty soldiers trudging out of the jungle. Someone in the room says, "That's me!" Someone else says, "Get the lights." Already there was too much emotion in the voices.

The lights went out, and as if on cue, the first pictures of bodies filled the scene. Someone in the room whispered an obscenity. Another veteran shouted an expletive. John Flynn, the CBS correspondent on the screen, said, "[t]he commander says the men of Charlie Company did nothing wrong…" and in the room, Marty Kroah buries his face in his hands and cries. Another man hurriedly left the room. The same veteran who had already shouted an obscenity does so again.

The narrator said something about machine guns in the trees, and Harold Hunter wailed. Wailed. "Oh yes, they had those Goddamned fifties [calibers]. We walked right into them." It takes everyone a moment to realize Harold was not shouting to the room. Harold was back in Vietnam. Harold was lying beneath the arc of a .51 caliber anti-aircraft machine gun that was blasting his friends to pieces. He was crying, his broad shoulders quaking. The video ended, but Harold did not. He screamed through his tears. His body was shaking. No one moved to him. It may have been that each man was back in Vietnam in that moment, shaking and crying with Harold. No one was embarrassed.

Finally, someone shouted, "Yeah but we kicked their ass!" Despite the total nonsense of such a statement, others confirmed the conclusion. "Yeah, we kicked their ass!"

Everyone seemed to feel better; even Harold stopped wailing. "We kicked their ass." And the lights came on, the drinking commenced again, and everyone lit a cigarette. The conversations began anew. The moment passed. Two couples talked about heading over to the Grand Ole Opry on Saturday. One veteran made his goodbyes because he had to catch a plane for California the following day.

The tattooed fiancée walked over to Harold Hunter. She asked him if he would like a beer. Hunter looked up. He said emphatically, "we kicked their ass'" but the tears continued to run down his face.

Charlie Company, 2/16, 1st Infantry Division Interviewees

Kenneth M. Alderson
Steve Antal, Jr.
John Babino
Charles Barnicoat (not at the battle)
Douglas D. Blankenheim
Alvin R. Brown
David E. Burris
Robert G. Canady (not at the battle)
Wesley R. Carpenter
Gilbert Delao
Smith Devoe A., Jr.
Peter F. A. Faberski
James W. Finney
Bob Lavery Fisher
John D. Fulford
Richard Garner
Klaus Grill (not at the battle)
Ronald Haley
Phillip J. Hall
Roger K. Harris
Robert J. Holton
Harold Hunter
Leonardus Inkelaar
Richard Jenkins (Not at the battle)
Daniel L. Kirby
Martin L. Kroah, Jr.
Milton L. Lader, Jr.
Douglas Landry
Johan J. Lang

Leroy Lark
John W. Libs
Leroy Love
Dave Marchetti
Kenneth R. Mize
Bill Moore (not at the Battle)
Charles F. Navarro
John A. Noyce
James R. Owens
Francis D. Peters
Ted L. Piner
Robert L. Rexroad
John Seville (Not at the battle, emails only)
Rolf Schoolman
David Stewart (not at the battle, emails only)
Galen Summerlot
Charles Urconis
Charles F. Weyant

Non-Charlie company interviewees

Francis Fox (Artillery forward observer, present at the battle)
Dennis Moorhead (Company A commander)
Bibb Underwood (battalion XO)
Jim Sutterfield (brother to Hugh Sutterfield)
Gerald Griffin (aid to General DePuy)

The Fallen Americans of Xa Cam My

PFC Marion F. Acton,
SP4 Howard C. Blevins,
PFC Carl D. Buckley,
PFC Andrew J. Campbell,
SGT William H. Causey,
SSGT Ralph Coleman,
PFC John A. Davis,
SP4 Donald E. Dermont Jr.,
PFC Dennis A. Desco,
PFC Philyaw Fee,
SP4 Eugene Garrett Jr.,
PFC Edward L. George,
SSGT Bozy Gerald,
PFC David A. Hammett,
PFC Charles E. Harvey,
PFC Norman L. Hawkins,
PFC Robert Allen Johnson,
SSGT Philip A. Jones,
PSGT Everett E. Langston,
SGT Richard J. Manley,
PVT Emmitt Mays Jr.,
SP4 Charles D. Oglesby,
A1C William H. Pitsenbarger
SP4 Randall B. Prinz,
PFC Edward W. Reilly,
SGT James W. Robinson, Jr.
SGT Ronald J. Seasholtz,
SP4 Henry A. Shiver,
PFC J.C. L. Short,
PFC Joseph F. Smith,

PFC Thomas D. Steele,
CPT George C. Steinberg,
PFC Deane S. Van Dyke Jr.,
PFC Daniel E. Walden,
PFC George H. Ward,
PFC John W. Watkins,
SGT Irving M. Wilson Jr

Bibliography

1967. "" Heliborne Operations,"." In *Vietnam, The First Year: A Pictorial History of the 2nd Brigade, 1st Infantry Division.*, unnumbered. Toykyo: Dai Nippon Printing Co.

2005. *"Bringing Smoke," Ready Now: Charlie Company 2/16.* Jan 13. http://www.angelfire.com/ar3/charlierangers/BringingSmoke.html.

1967. ""Fundamentals of Infantry Tactics,"." San Francisco 96345: Department of the Army, Headquarters 1st Infantry Division.

1966. "Artillery Support During Battle of Xa Cam My, 11 April, 1966," 1st Battalion, 7th Artillery, ALRDA-D, 19, April 1966." The Department of the Army, April 19.

Buzzanco, Robert. 1996. *Masters of War.* New York: Cambridge University Press. n.d. *Captain George C. Steinberg: Award of the Distinguished Service Cross. General Orders Number 191, HQ USARPAC,.* Accessed Nov 12, 2022. https://www.vvmf.org/Wall-of-Faces/49656/GEORGE-C-STEINBERG/.

Carland, John M. 2001. *Combat Operations: Stemming the Tide, May 1965 to October 1966.* Washington D.C: Government Reprints Press.

Chivalette, William I. and W. Parker Hayes, Jr. n.d. ""William H. Pitsenbarger: Third Enlisted Air Force Cross Recipient"." *The Airmen Heritage Series: The Airmen Memorial Museum.*

Clay, Steven. 2001. *Blood and Sacrifice; The History of the 16th Infantry Regiment From the Civil War Through the Gulf War.* Chicago: Cantigny First Division Foundation.

26 April 1966. "Combat After Action Report: Operation Abilene." Department of the Army, Headquarters 2d Brigade 1st Infantry Division.

DePuy, William. 1988. "Private letter to John Libs."

Derks, Tracy. Leesburg, VA: Primedia Publications, Vol 17, Number 4. ""Xa Cam My. Charlie Company's Longest Night"." *Vietnam Magazine*, Dec: 34-41.

Dunnigan, James F. and Albert A. Nofi. 1999. *Dirty Little Secrets of the Vietnam War.* New York: Thomas Dunne.

Fisher, Robert. 1971. ""Massacre on an Easter Monday"." *Graduate paper.*
—. n.d. "Term Paper."

Flynn, John. 1966. "News Report." *CBS News.* April 11.

Frisbee, John L. 1983. *"Valor: That Others Might Live," Air and Space Forces Magazine.* Oct 1. Accessed Nov 11, 2022. https://www.airandspaceforces.com/article/valor-that-others-may-live/.

Hackler, Will. 2021. *"Additional Family information," Facebook Messenger.* 4 16.

Haley, Ron. 2004. *"The Foxhole" Ready Now: Charlie Company 2/16.* Oct 22. Accessed November 11, 2022. http://www.angelfire.com/ar3/charlierangers/stories/Shovel.html.

Ham, Paul. 2010. *Vietnam: The Australian War.* Sydney: HarperCollins Publishers.

Harris, Roger. 2001. "Charlie's Kid, 1st edition." Roanoke: Unpublished Memoir.

Harrison, R. P. Fall, 2003. ""Mapping Jungle Trails"." unpublished manuscript.

Hay, John H. 1974. *Vietnam Studies: Tactical and Materiel Innovations.* Washington, D.C.: The Department of the Army.

Heber Springs Gazette. 1966. ""Silver Star Awarded Posthumously To Sgt. Everett Langston,"." April 15.

Herbert, Paul H. 1988. *Leavenworth Papers Number 16: Deciding What Has to Be Done: General William E. De Puy and the 1976 Edition of FM100-5, Operations.* Fort Leavenworth, Kansas:: Combat Studies Institute.

1966. *James William Robinson, Jr., Stories of Sacrifice, Congressional Medal of Honor Society .* Accessed November 12, 20 22 . https://www.cmohs.org/recipients/james-w-robinson-jr.

Kiernan, Ben. 2017. *Viet Nam: A History from the Earliest Times to the Present.* New York: Oxford University Press.

Kinnard, Douglas. 1977. *The War Managers: American Generals Reflect on Vietnam.* New York: Da Capo.

Krepinevich, Andrew F. Jr. 1986. *The Army and Vietnam .* Baltimore: The John Hopkins Univesity Press.

Lang, John. 2004. *"John Lang's Moving Wall," Ready Now: Charlie Company 2/16.* Oct 23. Accessed 11 11, 2022. https://www.angelfire.com/ar3/charlierangers/stories/LangsMovingWall.html.

Lanning, Michael Lee and Cragg, Dan. 1992. *Inside the VC and the NVA.* New York: Fawcett Columbine Book.

LaPointe, Robert. n.d. *"The Story of William Hart Pitsenbarger," PJ's in Vietnam.* Accessed 1 5, 2001.

http://www.pjsinnam.com/VN_History/Pitsenbarger/Pitsenbarger.htm.

McCrary, Lacy Dean. n.d. *WILLIAM H. PITSENBARGER: BRAVEST AMONG THE BRAVE VIETNAM WAR VETERAN, History.net.* Accessed Nov 11, 2022. https://www.historynet.com/william-h-pitsenbarger-bravest-among-the-brave-vietnam-war-veteran/.

McKay, Gary,. 2003. *Australia's Battlefields in Viet Nam.* Crow's Nest NSW: Allen & Unwin.

Milsten, Dave. April 12, 1966. " "Narrative – Rescue Mission --- Recovering Casualties from "C" Company, 2nd Battalion, 16th Infantry, 1st Infantry Division." . ." Department of the Air Force.

Milsten, Dave. 1999. *"Dedication of Pararescue Dorm" Speech.* Performed by Dave Milsten. Kirtland Air Force Base. Sept.

Mize, Ken. n.d. *"Xa Cam My: Three Views," Ready Now: Charlie Company 2/16 website, , accessed 1.13.2005.* Accessed Jan 13, 2005. http://www.angelfire.com/ar3/charlierangers/News/41103.html.

n.d. *Morning Reports 3.1.66 through 4.11.66, Company C, 2nd Bn/16th Inf. Regiment, 1st Infantry Division.* The Department of the Army.

N.A. n.d. *Narrative - The Battle of Xa Cam My.* The Department of the Army.

Navarro, Fred, and Robert Johnson, interview by Randi Barros and Dora Militaru. 2001. *"The Ripple Effect," Life 360, Randi Barros, editor, Dora Militaru, producer. Broadcast 10.04.2001.* (Oct. 10).

Nichols, Glenda Watkins Nichols. 2021. *Text Message.* 8 27.

Norton, Glenda Watkins. n.d. "Text Message."

O'Brien, Tim. 1990. *The Things They Carried.* Boston: Mariner Books.

Olson, James & Roberts, Randy. 1991. *Where the Dominos Fell.* New York: St. Martin's Press.

1967. "Pfc Deane Van Dyke, Jr., Award of the Bronze Star Medal , News Release, February, 1967." *News Release.* Department of the Army, Feb.

Reinberg, Linda. 1991. *In the Field: The Language of the Vietnam War.* Facts on File, Inc.

Robison, Donald R. 1985. ""The Enemy,"." In *Infantry in Vietnam: Small Unit Actions in the Early Days: 1965- 66,* by editor Albert N. Garland. New York: Jove Books.

Salem, Harold D. n.d. "Chronological Narrative (Statement)." (Recommendation for the Medal of Honor for William H. Pitsenbarger).

1966. "Sergeant John L. Bradley: Award of the Bronze Star Medal for Heroism. ." *General Orders Number 709.* Department of the Army, May 12.

1966. "Sergeant Robert Rexroad: Award of the Bronze Star Medal for Heroism. General Orders Number 737, May 20, 1966." *General Orders number 737.* Department of the Army, May.

Sheenan, Neill. 1988. *A Bright Shining Lie.* New York: Random House.

1966. "Specialist 4 Edward Lee George: Award of the Bronze Star Medal with the "V" Device. ." Department of the Army, May 23.

1966. "Specialist 4 Leonardus Inkelaar: Award of the Bronze Star Medal with the "V" Device. General Orders Number 737,." The Department of the Army, May 20.

Starry, Don A. 1980. *Armored Combat in Vietnam, (New York: Arno Press, 1980). 69.* New York: Arno Press.

Taylor, L. B., Jr. 1967. ""No-Retreat Super-Hero Who Stopped the Cong Cold"." *Stag Magazine*, November: 17, 84 - 87/.

Taylor, Sandra C. 1999. *Vietnamese Women at War: Fighting for Ho Chi Minh and the Revolution. .* Lawrence: University of Kansas Press.

Ward, Robert E., III. 1985. ""Keep An Eye on the Ball"." In *Infantry in Vietnam*, by ed. LTC Albert N. Garland, 159-163. New York: Jove Books.

Warren Wilkins. 2011. *Grab Their Belts to Fight Them: The Viet Cong's Big-Unit War Against the U.S., 1965-1966.* Annapolis: Annapolis, Naval Institute Press.

Westmoreland, William C.,. 1980. *A Soldier Reports.* New York: Dell Publishing Co., Inc.

Wilson, George C. 1989. *Mud Soldiers; Life inside the New American Army.* New York: Collier Books.

Woods, Andrew. 2006. ""40 years ago—Vietnam: 2/16th and the battle of Xa Cam My, 11 April 1966"." *Bridgehead Sentinel*, Spring: 6-7.

Notes

[1] (Westmoreland 1980) 232.
[2] (O'Brien 1990) 74.
[3] (O'Brien 1990) 74.
[4] (Fisher, "Massacre on an Easter Monday" 1971)
[5] (Harris, Charlie's Kid 2001) 11.
[6] (Fisher, "Massacre on an Easter Monday" 1971)
[7] (Harris, Charlie's Kid 2001) 11.
[8] (Wilson 1989) 10.
[9] (Fisher, "Massacre on an Easter Monday" 1971)
[10] (Wilson 1989) 11.
[11] (Warren Wilkins 2011) 193.
[12] (Harris, Charlie's Kid 2001) 11.
[13] (Wilson 1989) 12.
[14] (Wilson 1989) 11.
[15] (Ham 2010) Kindle Location 3443.
[16] (" Heliborne Operations," 1967) unnumbered.
[17] (Combat After Action Report: Operation Abilene 26 April 1966)
— (Carland 2001) 306.
[18] (Sheenan 1988) 382.
— (Buzzanco 1996) 220.
[19] (Kinnard 1977) 40-41.
[20] (Carland 2001) 165.
[21] (Carland 2001) 51.
[22] (Sheenan 1988) 619.
[23] (Olson 1991) 115.
[24] (Carland 2001) 356.
[25] (Carland 2001) 358.
[26] (Woods, "40 years ago—Vietnam: 2/16th and the battle of Xa Cam My, 11 April 1966" 2006)
[27] (" Heliborne Operations," 1967) unnumbered.
[28] (Wilson 1989) 15.
[29] (Fisher, "Massacre on an Easter Monday" 1971)
[30] (" Heliborne Operations," 1967)
[31] (Wilson 1989) 10-11.
[32] (Narrative - The Battle of Xa Cam My n.d.)

[33] (Narrative - The Battle of Xa Cam My n.d.)
[34] (Harris, Charlie's Kid 2001) 12.
[35] (Morning Reports 3.1.66 through 4.11.66, Company C, 2nd Bn/16th Inf. Regiment, 1st Infantry Division n.d.)
[36] (Morning Reports 3.1.66 through 4.11.66, Company C, 2nd Bn/16th Inf. Regiment, 1st Infantry Division n.d.)
[37] (Reinberg 1991) 84.
[38] (Westmoreland 1980) 187.
[39] (Wilson 1989) 17.
[40] (Harrison Fall, 2003)
[41] (Wilson 1989) 16.
[42] (Wilson 1989) 17.
[43] (Wilson 1989) 17.
[44] (Wilson 1989) 14.
[45] (Narrative - The Battle of Xa Cam My n.d.)
[46] (Wilson 1989) 17.
[47] (Harris, Charlie's Kid 2001) 12.
[48] (Fisher, "Massacre on an Easter Monday" 1971)
[49] (Sergeant Robert Rexroad: Award of the Bronze Star Medal for Heroism. General Orders Number 737, May 20, 1966. 1966)
[50] (Narrative - The Battle of Xa Cam My n.d.)
 (Wilson 1989) 17.
[51] (Harris, Charlie's Kid 2001) 12.
[52] (Warren Wilkins 2011) 193.
[53] (L. B. Taylor 1967) 84.
[54] (Harrison Fall, 2003)
[55] (Dunnigan 1999) 61.
[56] (Warren Wilkins 2011)
[57] (Hay, Vietnam Studies: Tactical and Materiel Innovations, (Washington D.C.: , 1974.) 1974) 61.
[58] ("Fundamentals of Infantry Tactics," 1967)
[59] (Herbert 1988) 20
[60] (Carland 2001) 360
[61] (Krepinevich 1986) 190.
[62] (Krepinevich 1986) 167.
[63] (Carland 2001)161.
[64] (Combat After Action Report: Operation Abilene 26 April 1966) 2.
[65] (Combat After Action Report: Operation Abilene 26 April 1966) 3.
[66] (Combat After Action Report: Operation Abilene 26 April 1966) 3.
[67] (Robison 1985)

[68] (Warren Wilkins 2011) 191.
[69] (Combat After Action Report: Operation Abilene 26 April 1966) 3.
[70] (Warren Wilkins 2011) 192.
[71] (Warren Wilkins 2011) 193
[72] (Combat After Action Report: Operation Abilene 26 April 1966) 3.
[73] (Combat After Action Report: Operation Abilene 26 April 1966) 3.
[74] (Warren Wilkins 2011) 192-193.
[75] (Derks, "Xa Cam My. Charlie Company's Longest Night" Leesburg, VA: Primedia Publications, Vol 17, Number 4) 37.
[76] (Derks, "Xa Cam My. Charlie Company's Longest Night" Leesburg, VA: Primedia Publications, Vol 17, Number 4) 37
[77] (Combat After Action Report: Operation Abilene 26 April 1966) 3.
[78] (Wilson 1989) 19
[79] (Sergeant John L. Bradley: Award of the Bronze Star Medal for Heroism. 1966)
[80] (Haley 2004)
[81] (Lang 2004)
[82] (McCrary n.d.) 21.
[83] (Milsten, "Dedication of Pararescue Dorm" Speech 1999)
[84] (Salem n.d.) 2.
[85] (Salem n.d.) 2.
[86] (Salem n.d.) 2.
[87] (Salem n.d.) 2.
[88] (Salem n.d.) 3.
[89] (Fisher, "Massacre on an Easter Monday" 1971)
[90] (Milsten April 12, 1966)
[91] (Milsten, "Dedication of Pararescue Dorm" Speech 1999)
[92] (Chivalette n.d.)
[93] (Frisbee 1983)
[94] (Salem n.d.) 3.
[95] (Milsten April 12, 1966)
[96] (McCrary n.d.)
[97] (Derks, "Xa Cam My. Charlie Company's Longest Night" Leesburg, VA: Primedia Publications, Vol 17, Number 4) 38.
[98] (Derks, "Xa Cam My. Charlie Company's Longest Night" Leesburg, VA: Primedia Publications, Vol 17, Number 4) 38.
[99] (Wilson 1989) 20
[100] (Wilson 1989) 20
[101] (Derks, "Xa Cam My. Charlie Company's Longest Night" Leesburg, VA: Primedia Publications, Vol 17, Number 4) 39.

[102] ("Silver Star Awarded Posthumously To Sgt. Everett Langston," 1966)
[103] (Wilson 1989) 23.
[104] (Specialist 4 Edward Lee George: Award of the Bronze Star Medal with the "V" Device. 1966)
[105] (Captain George C. Steinberg: Award of the Distinguished Service Cross. General Orders Number 191, HQ USARPAC, n.d.)
[106] ("Silver Star Awarded Posthumously To Sgt. Everett Langston," 1966)
[107] (Pfc Deane Van Dyke, Jr., Award of the Bronze Star Medal, News Release, February, 1967 1967)
[108] (Wilson 1989) 25.
[109] (Specialist 4 Edward Lee George: Award of the Bronze Star Medal with the "V" Device. 1966)
[110] (Captain George C. Steinberg: Award of the Distinguished Service Cross. General Orders Number 191, HQ USARPAC, n.d.)
[111] (Captain George C. Steinberg: Award of the Distinguished Service Cross. General Orders Number 191, HQ USARPAC, n.d.)
[112] (Wilson 1989) 25.
[113] (Nichols 2021)
[114] (Wilson 1989) 25.
[115] (Wilson 1989) 28-29.
[116] (Clay 2001) 284.
[117] ("Bringing Smoke," Ready Now: Charlie Company 2/16 2005)
[118] (Mize n.d.)
 -(Hackler 2021)
[119] (Derks, "Xa Cam My. Charlie Company's Longest Night" Leesburg, VA: Primedia Publications, Vol 17, Number 4) 40.
[120] (Derks, "Xa Cam My. Charlie Company's Longest Night" Leesburg, VA: Primedia Publications, Vol 17, Number 4) 40.
[121] (Sergeant John L. Bradley: Award of the Bronze Star Medal for Heroism. 1966)
 -(Specialist 4 Leonardus Inkelaar: Award of the Bronze Star Medal with the "V" Device. General Orders Number 737, 1966)
[122] (Woods, "40 years ago—Vietnam: 2/16th and the battle of Xa Cam My, 11 April 1966" 2006)
[123] (Fisher, "Massacre on an Easter Monday" 1971)
[124] (Harris, Charlie's Kid 2001) 13.
[125] (Harris, Charlie's Kid 2001) 14.
[126] (Woods, "40 years ago—Vietnam: 2/16th and the battle of Xa Cam My, 11 April 1966" 2006)
[127] (Wilson 1989) 26.

[128] (Wilson 1989) 26-27.
[129] (McCrary n.d.)
[130] (Navarro 2001)
[131] (McCrary n.d.)
[132] (Derks, "Xa Cam My. Charlie Company's Longest Night" Leesburg, VA: Primedia Publications, Vol 17, Number 4) 41.
[133] (Wilson 1989) 31.
[134] (Wilson 1989) 31.
[135] (Artillery Support During Battle of Xa Cam My, 11 April, 1966," 1st Battalion, 7th Artillery, ALRDA-D, 19, April 1966 1966)
[136] (Fisher, "Massacre on an Easter Monday" 1971)
[137] (Warren Wilkins 2011) 38, 39.
[138] (S. C. Taylor 1999) 74.
[139] (Kiernan 2017) 78.
(Ham, Vietnam: The Australian War 2010) Kindle Location 192-195.
[140] (Narrative - The Battle of Xa Cam My n.d.) 4.
[141] (Harris, Charlie's Kid 2001) 14.
[142] (Wilson 1989) 30
[143] (Narrative - The Battle of Xa Cam My n.d.)
[144] (Wilson 1989) 37.
[145] (Narrative - The Battle of Xa Cam My n.d.) 4.
[146] (Warren Wilkins 2011) 194.
[147] (Warren Wilkins 2011) 194.
[148] (Harris, Charlie's Kid 2001) 14.
[149] (Harris, Charlie's Kid 2001) 14.
[150] (Narrative - The Battle of Xa Cam My n.d.) 4.
[151] (LaPointe n.d.)
[152] (Harris, Charlie's Kid 2001) 15.
[153] (Fisher, "Massacre on an Easter Monday" 1971)
[154] (Flynn 1966)
[155] (Flynn 1966)
[156] (Flynn 1966)
[157] (Harris, Charlie's Kid 2001) 15.
[158] (Flynn 1966)
[159] (Ward 1985) 163.
[160] (Ward 1985) 163.
[161] (Ward 1985)
[162] (DePuy 1988)
[163] (Wilson 1989) 24
[164] (Harrison Fall, 2003) 1.

[165] (Combat After Action Report: Operation Abilene 26 April 1966)
[166] (Carland 2001) 175, 358.
[167] (DePuy 1988)
[168] (Starry 1980) 69.
[169] (Wilson 1989) 38.
[170] (DePuy 1988)
[171] (Kinnard 1977) 66.
[172] (Warren Wilkins 2011) 192.

CPSIA information can be obtained
at www.ICGtesting.com
Printed in the USA
LVHW081104180323
741932LV00016B/956